The Plague Reconsidered

A new look at its origins and effects in 16th and 17th Century England

A Local Population Studies Supplement

Published by 'Local Population Studies' in association with the S.S.R.C. Cambridge Group for the History of Population and Social Structure.

About this book

The plague reconsidered: a new look at its origins and effects in sixteenth and seventeenth century England is the fourth *Local Population Studies* supplement. The idea for this book emerged from an attempt to compile from readers' contributions a series of notes and comments on plague in Britain for publication in *Local Population Studies*. For a number of reasons these plague notes never reached the pages of *LPS* but from this experience we came to realise both how widespread is the ignorance and confusion about the causes and spread of plague and its implications for the economic or local historian and for the historical demographer, and how many problems there are which still await resolution. With the intention of casting new light on these unresolved issues and of making some of the recent research on plague more easily available to the non-specialist reader, we have brought together in this volume original case studies and articles which review, assess and synthesise other important work.

The case studies examine plague epidemics in Bristol, Eyam and Colyton and we also include in a further case study an attempt to interpret the geographical spread of plague, based on evidence of the London plague of 1603. Two articles consider the medical and epidemiological aspects of plague, one of these being a translation of a chapter of Noel Biraben's recent outstanding contribution to the subject, *Les hommes et la peste*. We also include a review of J.F.D. Shrewsbury's *A history of bubonic plague in the British Isles* and an article which describes some of the erroneous views of plague which have crept into even some of the better-known books produced for school use and for the general reader.

It is our belief that this book contains material which will make a substantial contribution towards a better understanding of plague in sixteenth and seventeenth century England. It will therefore be essential reading for the specialist but one of the principal objectives of *Local Population Studies* is to illuminate the more difficult areas of demographic history for the non-specialist and the amateur, and in this supplement we hope we have succeeded in serving their needs by providing them with an authoritative guide and an insight into what is a complex but fascinating subject.

Local Population Studies
Editorial Board
April 1977

Contents

Paul Slack is Fellow and Tutor in Modern History at Exeter College, Oxford. His publications include *English Towns in Transition 1500 – 1700* (with P. Clark) and an edition of documents, *Poverty in early Stuart Salisbury*. He is at present completing a book on the impact of plague in Tudor and Stuart England.

Leslie Bradley has been working for some years on Demographic studies of Derbyshire parishes and on the effects of epidemic diseases, such as smallpox and plague.

Jean-Noel Biraben is a qualified doctor now working with the National Institute of Demography in Paris.

Christopher Morris is a Fellow of King's College, Cambridge, and was formerly lecturer in History in the University of Cambridge.

Roger Schofield is a co-director of the S.S.R.C. Cambridge Group for the History of Population and Social Structure.

Derek Turner teaches at Christ's Hospital Horsham, as Head of the History Department. He undertook post-graduate study at Oxford on sixteenth and seventeenth century historical demography with particular reference to plague. He has written l*Historical Demography in Schools* and a number of articles in *Local Population Studies* and other periodicals.

'The editors would like to thank David Avery for compiling the index and to acknowledge the co-operation of the Mansell Collection, the British Museum and the Bodleian Library in making illustrations available for this publication.'

Introduction

Paul Slack

The history of epidemics of plague and pestilence has always attracted attention. From the Black Death of 1348-9 to the 'Great Plague' of the 1660s these disasters filled the pages of contemporary annals of most English towns, they were commemorated by tablets in parish churches, and they were studied with some sophistication by the first English demographers from John Graunt onwards. In recent years with new advances in historical studies they have become of more central interest to historians both amateur and professional. The schoolteacher can scarcely avoid discussing the dramatic events of 1348 and 1665. Neither can literary, economic or political historians ignore the impact of epidemics of plague on their own concerns. Practitioners in the fields of local history and historical demography, whose interests are mirrored in the pages of *Local Population Studies,* are often confronted by periods of crisis mortality and are increasingly using parish registers in order to understand and interpret those which occurred after 1538. For those who read history and those who try to write it plague is a subject of interest and importance.

It is also, however, a controversial and a difficult one, and this explains many of the deficiencies and ambiguities which pervade the existing historical literature. Not only are school textbooks inadequate and sometimes inaccurate on the subject, as Turner's article in this collection shows,[1] but even the specialist literature on plague is often confusing and contradictory. As recent studies have demonstrated, there is little agreement on the criteria for identifying historical epidemics of bubonic plague, on the nature of their incidence or on their demographic or social effects. The aim of the editors of *Local Population Studies* in bringing together this collection has therefore been to illustrate and provide a guide to the complexities of the subject for those whose interest has been aroused by their research or their reading. It does not provide simple solutions, for these are not yet within sight. Some of the problems can be resolved only by detailed local investigation, and the second aim of this collection is to illustrate the sort of work which can be undertaken and the significance of the results which may emerge. Plague is an important subject, but also still an uncertain and a demanding one, where local studies can be of real service.

The most obviously difficult task for the historian is to identify the diseases at work in periods of high mortality and hence to try to form reliable hypotheses about the ways in which they spread and the effects they might be expected to produce. He wants to be able to name the epidemic and to use modern experience of it as an aid to interpreting the partial evidence which survives for past outbreaks. But this is easier said than done. Even the work of historians with specialist medical training can be unreliable. It may be heavily influenced, for example, by the wish to prove a particular thesis. This has been shown to be the case with Creighton's classic *History of Epidemics,* in which the historical evidence was selected to support the author's miasmatic theory that epidemics were a result of poisonous emanations from the soil.[2] Morris's review printed below applies comparable criticisms to Shrewsbury's recent attempt to revise parts of Creighton's work.[3] Certainly a reading of standard medical textbooks on plague, that of Pollitzer for example,[4] suggests that the disease is much more complicated and much less completely understood than historians have often supposed and than Shrewsbury's book would lead them to believe. Indeed the complex nature and epidemiology of plague,.and the ways in which past European epidemics may have differed from some modern Asian ones, have been further illuminated by medical research undertaken in the twenty years since Pollitzer's work appeared. Recent contributions to specialist knowledge of the different kinds of plague are, however, summarized in the chapter by a distinguished French authority. Biraben, printed below, and the areas of doubt and certainty relevant to students of the past are discussed in Bradley's essay.[5]

In addition to the medical uncertainties, there are also problems of historical evidence. Since contemporary descriptions of the symptoms exhibited by past diseases are hard to find, it is seldom possible to determine with confidence whether a particular period of crisis mortality was caused by bubonic plague or by some other epidemic disease, whether typhus, smallpox or influenza. If the crisis was a particularly severe one, the historian may be helped by the characteristic chronological incidence of major outbreaks of bubonic plague, in which mortality reaches a peak in the late summer or autumn and declines with the onset of colder weather, and by its tendency, in the early modern period at any rate, to have a marked family incidence, several deaths occurring in household groups, whole families sometimes disappearing.[6] But if the number of burials is more evenly spread over the year, as sometimes happens even in epidemics of plague, the problem of identity is more intractable. Historians are liable to disagree and the question has to be left open.[7]

If an outbreak of bubonic plague can be tentatively identified, however, a second set of problems arises with regard to the means by which it was transmitted. Whether plague was contagious or not was a question which preoccupied some of the earliest observers of epidemics,[8] and in spite of the understanding of the role of the black rat and its flea as carriers of the disease which came at the end of the nineteenth century, the subject still poses problems. The vital question here is whether the human flea as well as the rat flea was important as a vector in historical epidemics. Much recent work would suggest that it was, that plague might be transmitted in this way from individual to individual without the intervention of the rat, and that this accounts for the heavy family incidence of the disease in the past[9]. If this argument is accepted, it has wider implications. It would affect, for example, our assessment of the quarantine measures so widely adopted against plague in the sixteenth and seventeenth centuries. For if it was the movement of men which was primarily responsible for carrying the disease from place to place, the black rat being essentially sedentary in its habits, and if it was the human flea which transmitted the disease from person to person, then *cordons sanitaires* and quarantine of those infected may well have played a part in limiting and in the end stamping out plague in western Europe. Biraben has argued this case strongly.[10] But it depends, as he is aware, not only on medical assumptions but also on historical judgements about the administrative efficiency of public health measures in the seventeenth century, a topic on which there is room for disagreement and for more local research.[11]

Another area of controversy related to this, and again one which exercised seventeenth-century writers, concerns the origin of the great epidemics of plague. Could the disease persist among rodent populations in temperate countries like England during the intervals between epidemics, or were these outbreaks normally begun by its introduction from outside? Morris and Shrewsbury are at odds on this,[12] although the importance of ports like London, Yarmouth and Exeter in the origins of English epidemics points in the direction of importation. But only careful work tracing the spread of epidemics of plague will help us to determine the facts about any particular outbreak.[13]

It might seem that such technical problems relating to the epidemiology and aetiology of plague, or for that matter of other diseases, are of only peripheral interest to the historian concerned with the effects rather than the causes of high mortality. As the example of quarantine shows, however, this would be a short-sighted view. For these problems often impinge on central questions of demographic and social history. One of the most interesting and important historical developments of recent years has been the attention paid to what the French have termed 'crises of subsistence', those periods in preindustrial European history when bad harvests, high prices and high mortality rates coincided and seem to have been related.[14] In any serious discussion of this subject it is necessary to try to identify the diseases at work, to discover whether they were the sort of epidemics often associated with malnutrition in more modern societies, typhus, relapsing fever or pellagra for example, or whether they were outbreaks of bubonic plague which need not have had a causal connection with food shortages. As A.B. Appleby has shown, work on local parish registers may contribute a great deal to the investigation of this problem.[15]

It is related to a subject of even broader historical significance, the causes of long-term population movements in the past. The relevance of epidemic disease to this topic had been shown in a fresh and typically stimulating way in J.D. Chambers' book *Population, Economy and Society in Pre-industrial England*. He suggests that long-term demographic trends may often have been caused, not by fluctuations of a Malthusian kind in the balance between population levels and food supplies, but by independent biological changes in the virulence of disease, by the rise and fall of the great epidemic scourges, which were not economic in origin.[16] Chambers' arguments for the importance of this 'autonomous death-rate', as he describes it, deserve to be taken seriously, and they need to be tested by work on the changing severity of epidemic disease in the past and its relationship with variations in standards of living. The same general problem often arises at a more detailed level, for example in any consideration of the vexed question of why plague disappeared from England after the 1670s and from Western Europe in the early eighteenth century. Was this a consequence of economic change, of improvements in hygiene and living standards, or of a biological change in the nature of the plague bacillus? Or was it related to quite different factors, such as new methods of isolation and quarantine?[17]

The epidemiology of bubonic plague is a subject which bears on some of the central issues of demographic and social history therefore. It is equally relevant for the work of local historians trying to reconstruct a small community over a short period. Their analysis of the chronological pattern and the intensity of periods of high mortality in different places will benefit from an appreciation of the possible diseases involved and the ways in which they were spread, and will in turn help to advance our understanding of them. But plague is also a subject to which the local historian can make his own distinctive contribution. In particular it is only in the context of the local community that the immediate impact and the consequences of epidemics of plague can properly be examined. The studies of Colyton and Eyam below show the sort of results which can be obtained from analyses in depth.[18] But simpler comparisons of fluctuations in burials can provide indications of the severity of plague in different areas of the country at different times, which require further investigation.[19] Similar methods can be used to measure the relative levels of mortality in different social groups in major towns like Bristol.[20] Given its dependence on rats and fleas, it is not surprising to find that plague had its worst effects among the poor, but we do not yet know whether this socially selective incidence was as marked in smaller villages and market towns as in large cities.

The age and sex incidence of plague mortality are equally important elements in any assessment of the results of epidemics. In modern outbreaks both appear to fluctuate according to the exposure of different groups to infection,[21] and there may have been similar interesting variations in different preindustrial English communities. As far as age is concerned, it seems likely that, given normally high infant mortality rates, the effects of plague were most noticeable among older children and adolescents, but we cannot yet be more precise than this. In a recent article the Hollingsworths have produced some interesting calculations of mortality by age and sex during plague epidemics in one London parish. One important conclusion is that male mortality was much heavier than female, as some contemporary observers suggested.[22] If this was generally true, it has been argued that it may have had an influence on the balance between the sexes, keeping the sex ratio low, in seventeenth-century England.[23] But we need more local studies of this kind before we can begin to generalize from the experience of one metropolitan parish, for the Eyam evidence suggests that the pattern of plague mortality there was rather different.[24]

N.B.

All these possible variations in the incidence of plague affect one of the local historian's most pressing problems, the effects of epidemic crises on the long-term population history of local communities. Heavy mortality among adolescents might be expected to affect marriages and births and hence population trends for at least a generation. It is important therefore to try to trace the mechanism by which a parish or town recovered from an epidemic. It has been evident to demographers since the time of Graunt that heavy immigration allowed the population of London to rise despite successive epidemics.[25] But Bradley's research on Eyam summarized below shows how a close study of a smaller community can illuminate the processes of recovery, and demonstrates that there was migration into villages as well as towns after an outbreak of plague. His work suggests that in many instances the local effects of epidemic crises might be only temporary.[26]

In spite of the technical problems and historical controversies with which it is surrounded, the history of plague is of the first importance for the historical demographer and the local historian. It also has the virtue that its study, at whatever level, is related to wider problems of social and economic history. For Graunt and his successors the analysis of burial registers and bills of mortality was one means of measuring the quality of life in different parts of the country; and the study of the incidence of plague still has much to tell us about differences in living standards in different villages and towns or parts of a town. The ways in which the disease was spread and in which towns recovered their populations throw light on patterns of mobility and migration in a society which, we are beginning to realise, was by no means static. The panics and other reactions which epidemics of plague elicited, and the impact they have had on popular histories, chronicles and works of fiction, need to be set against a careful examination of the local evidence for mortality, as Bradley's study of the notorious case of Eyam shows. The study of epidemics of plague demands care and some knowledge of technicalities, but it should not result simply in the compilation of such collections of instances as Creighton and Shrewsbury undertook. For it is intimately related to the broader concerns of modern social and economic history. If this collection of essays encourages the more informed investigation of this particular demographic phenomenon, it will have helped to contribute to that wider study, and it will have served its purpose.

Notes

1. Below, pp. 133-141.
2. See R.S. Roberts, 'Epidemics and Social History', *Medical History* 12 (1968), 305–16, a review of C. Creighton, *A History of Epidemics in Britain* (reprinted with introductory material, 1965), originally published in 1891–4.
3. Below, pp. 37-47.
4. R. Pollitzer, *Plague,* 1954
5. Below, pp. 11-23
6. Cf. J.F.D. Shrewsbury, *A History of Bubonic Plague in the British Isles,* 1970, pp. 157, 181.
7. See for example the disagreement noted in A.B. Appleby, 'Disease or Famine? Mortality in Cumberland and Westmorland 1580-1640', *Econ. H. R.,* 2 Ser. XXVI (1973), 424, 429, and note.
8. Cf. L.F. Hirst, *The Conquest of Plague,* 1953, ch. III; C.F. Mullett, *The Bubonic Plague and England,* 1956.
9. Below, pp. 14-16; R.S. Roberts, 'The Uses of Literary and Documentary Evidence in the History of Medicine', in *Modern Methods in the History of Medicine,* ed. E. Clarke, 1971, p. 42.
10. See J-N. Biraben's remarks in *Problèmes de Mortalité,* ed. P. Harsin and E. Helin (Liege, 1965), pp. 19–22; he develops the case in his book, *Les hommes et la peste,* from which the chapter below is taken.
11. I hope to consider the development of public health measures against plague and their social implications in England in detail in a forthcoming book.
12. Below, pp. 41, 42
13. Some of the difficulties involved in such work are described in the article below, pp. 127-132
14. J. Meuvret, 'Demographic Crisis in France from the 16th to the 18th Century', in *Population in History,* ed. D.V. Glass and D.E.C. Eversley, 1965, pp. 507-22; P. Laslett, *The World We Have Lost,* 1965, ch. 5.
15. Appleby, 'Disease or Famine?'
16. J.D. Chambers, *Population, Economy and Society in Pre-industrial England,* 1972, ch. 4.
17. Cf. below, pp. 20, 21
18. Below, pp. 63-126
19. See R.S. Schofield, 'Crisis Mortality', LPS, 9, 1972, 10-21.
20. Cf. below, pp. 49-62
21. Pollitzer, *Plague,* pp. 503-4

22. M.F. and T.H. Hollingsworth, 'Plague Mortality Rates by Age and Sex in the Parish of St. Botolph's without Bishopsgate, London, 1603', *Population Studies,* XXV (1971), 131-46.
23. See the rather sweeping suggestions in R. Thompson, *Women in Stuart England and America,* 1974, esp. ch. 2.
24.. Below, p. 73.
25. Cf. E.A. Wrigley, 'A Simple Model of London's Importance in Changing English Society and Economy 1650-1750', *Past and Present,* no. 37 (1967), 46-49.
26. Below, pp. 74, 77.

'Townspeople fleeing into the country from the plague of 1630'

Some Medical Aspects of Plague

Leslie Bradley

The picture of plague and of its effects on population which has been presented by the historians has, up to the present, been oversimplified and misleading. Dogmatic statements have been made about, for example, the mode of transmission of plague and the degree of mortality which it causes, often without any realisation of the complexity of the plague phenomenon and of the strong differences of opinion which still exist among the medical experts. Only quite recently have these aspects of plague received attention in papers in the historical journals and it took the invasion of the historians' field by Professor J.F.D. Shrewsbury, a bacteriologist who roundly declared that the historians' ignorance of the epidemiology of plague has led them into serious errors, together with the reply by Mr. Christopher Morris, to convince historians and demographers in general that a proper understanding of the medical literature is essential to any proper study of the historical plagues.

Major difficulties, of course, have been that there is at present no publication which sets out at all clearly and concisely the present state of the medical views on plague and that it is difficult to estimate whether views gathered from experience of plague in, say, China are valid for plague in Britain between the fourteenth and the seventeenth centuries. The literature is voluminous and sometimes conflicting[1]. This brief account must, therefore, considerably simplify but not, I hope, falsify the main issues.

The development of the bacteriological and epidemiological theory

Although bacteriological science had been developing rapidly since the middle of the nineteenth century and Koch, for example, had discovered the causative bacteria of tuberculosis and cholera in the early 1880s, it was still possible for Creighton, in his great *History of Epidemics in Britain*[2] in 1894, to deny the bacteriological theory of infectious diseases and ascribe them to 'miasmata rising from the soil.' But he was fighting a losing rearguard action for, even as he wrote, the role of bacilli in infectious disease was widely regarded as well established.

The bacillus responsible for plague, *Pasteurella pestis* or, in more recent terminolgy, *Yersinia pestis,* was discovered by Yersin in 1894. At this point it must be said that there are two main types of plague, bubonic plague, the more frequent and popularly better known, and pneumonic plague. Both are caused by the same bacillus. Within each type there are less frequent variants, notably the acute septicaemic form of bubonic plague, described later.

In the early 1890s, too, the high mortality rate in rats which had been observed to accompany, or just precede, outbreaks of human plague was discovered to be due to the plague bacillus and it was soon widely, though not universally, accepted that bubonic plague is primarily a disease of rodents which may sometimes be transmitted to man though the method of transmission was for some time obscure. By 1908, the overwhelming importance of the flea as the transmitter of bubonic plague from rodents (and especially rats) to man had been demonstrated and the primary role assigned to the rat-flea *Xenopsylla cheopis*. After further investigation, the generally accepted theory of transmission was that a rat-flea, feeding on the blood of a rat host heavily infected by the plague bacillus, ingests bacilli which may multiply to such an extent in its stomach that they completely block the proventriculus, a valve-like organ at the entrance to the stomach. Such a flea is called a 'blocked' flea. If, usually owing, to the death of the normal rat host, a blocked flea transfers to a human host and attempts to take a meal of blood, the blood cannot pass the blocked proventriculus and is regurgitated under the human skin, carrying with it plague bacilli which may multiply and cause bubonic plague, so called because a common and prominent symptom is a bubo, a swelling of one of the lymphatic glands. Some rat fleas, and also the human flea *Pulex irritans,* have no proventriculus and transmission is by the contaminated proboscis, a much less efficient method of transmission. In either case, according to this theory, bubonic plague is not transmitted from man to man but only from rat to man. Shrewsbury suggests that the black rat was not present in England in sufficient numbers to sustain a plague epidemic until the thirteenth century (pp11-13).

This theory is not without its opponents and indeed, seventy years after Yersin's discovery, the medical literature of plague abounds in controversy. In their great treatises, Wu Lien-Teh and Pollitzer tend to make qualified statements such as: 'While it is generally admitted that plague-infected fleas may be carried on the person, or in the baggage, of travellers, opinions vary considerably as to the frequency and consequently the epidemiological importance of such a transport' (Pollitzer p.386)·and they give the evidence on both sides. Other writers, as we shall see, are more dogmatic. Some differences are, of course, due to differing local conditions, but even if we confine ourselves, as I now propose to do, to conditions obtaining in England up to the end of the seventeenth century, there are differences which are important for the historical discussion of plague.

Pneumonic Plague

But first it is necessary to say something about pneumonic plague. Once this form of plague is established, it is highly infectious and is transmitted directly from man to man, without any intermediary, through infected droplets expelled from the lungs during speech or coughing. There is disagreement as to whether, in Europe, pneumonic plague can originate only from a bubonic patient who contracts secondary pneumonia or whether primary pneumonic plague can arise without a bubonic origin. Wu Lien-Teh writes: "Whilst admitting the existence of 'original' pneumonic plagues, we must state emphatically that they are not the rule. The rule is that pneumonic plague arises from bubonic plague with secondary lung involvement" (p.163). Pollitzer (p.505) and Hirst (p.222) make similar statements. Shrewsbury says bluntly: 'Pneumonic plague cannot exist in the absence of the bubonic form and it cannot persist as an independent form of plague' (p.6). Once it has arisen pneumonic plague can spread very rapidly, can be carried from one place to another by an infected person and, until recently, was almost invariably fatal. This is important in the controversy over the extent of the mortality caused by the great plague epidemic of 1349, later named the Black Death. Shrewsbury is concerned to demonstrate that the commonly accepted estimates are far too high. Morris attacks this thesis, writing; ' But for some reason he has chosen to turn a blind eye to any evidence of pneumonic plague. He does not notice how often the victims are said to have succumbed in three days... ' (p.207). The point is, of course that the case-fatality rate of pneumonic plague is very much higher than that of the bubonic form. Wu Lien-Teh, however, writes: ' It is necessary to emphasise the large part which bubonic plague played in the Black Death, because it is occasionally mentioned as being purely pneumonic. It can be gathered from the records of contemporary writers that the pneumonic type was most prevalent at the beginning of many local outbreaks, that only in some localities did it continue to rage in this form, and that most often it assumed the bubonic character after a few months... We have seen that pneumonic plague played its most important role at the beginning of the Black Death. As far as we can see, this seems to have subsided quickly, and even permanently in some affected localities ' (pp3-6) Nor does it follow that a high percentage of deaths within three days rules out a bubonic form of plague as Morris implies. Biraben suggests that ' in the bubonic form we can reckon on the average that one percent to two percent die suddenly, thirty to forty percent before the second day ', though these estimates are a good deal higher than those made by other writers. Pollitzer, for example, says: ' Though it may take place sooner or later, death during the acute stage of bubonic plague usually takes place within a period of three to five days from the onset of illness, so that patients who survive longer than five days have considerably increased chances of recovery ' (p.418). In the acute septicaemic form of bubonic plague, the degree of infection by the bacillus is so high that the patient succumbs from a generalised infection before the normal plague symptoms such as the bubo have had time to develop. On the other hand though septicaemic plague has a very high case-fatality rate it is, according to Hirst, less infectious than pneumonic plague (p.29) and so would be likely to cause fewer deaths.

There appears to be general agreement that the epidemics of the sixteenth and seventeenth centuries were of the bubonic form.

Which Flea?

Reverting now to the more common bubonic plague, the medical disagreement of importance to the historical discussion concerns the flea. Which flea was the vector responsible for the promotion of plague epidemics in Britain? If, as has been generally accepted, it was a rodent flea, it must have been one which has as its host one of the 'commensal' rodents, those which frequent human settlements. Alternatively, it may have been a human flea, though other parasites such as the body louse have been shown to be capable of playing a minor role. Of the rodent fleas, the two possibilities for Britain appear to be *Xenopsylla Cheopis* and *Nosopsylla fasciatus*. Over the world as a whole, *X. cheopis* has usually been assigned the major role though, in varying local conditions, other fleas may be more important. Pollitzer, however, 'finds it difficult to believe that *X. cheopis* was rampant there (i.e. in north-west Europe) in the past' (p.373), though his reasons (pp327-332) do not appear to me to be very convincing. His argument is that it is most prevalent in warm countries: 'a moderately warm and moist climate is optimal for *X. cheopis.*' At the same time, 'as shown by its wide geographical distribution, *X. cheopis* is able to adapt itself to a considerable range of climatic conditions. It is, as has been previously noted, the common rat-flea in Manchuria', though he ascribes its frequency in Manchuria to 'the peculiar heating arrangements in many of the houses.' Accepting Pollitzer's thesis would leave us with *N. fasciatus* and the human flea *Pulex irritans*. Both have been shown to be capable of transmitting plague, though considerably less effectively than *X. cheopis*. Pollitzer 'is led to believe that *N. fasciatus* and *P. irritans* were responsible for the spread of infection in the historical outbreaks of north-west Europe. No doubt exists that these pests abounded then, so that their large numbers might have compensated for any shortcomings in their vector capacity' (p373). He quotes Eskey as laying stress 'upon the fact that the extrinsic incubation period was much longer in the case of *N. fasciatus* than in that of *X. cheopis*. In his opinion plague outbreaks in warm countries, where *X. cheopis* was the vector, ran a rapid course with a high incidence of human infection. In colder climates, where *N. fasciatus* preponderated, the outbreaks were prolonged and the incidence of human plague was low' (p.372). He adds, however, that 'one should beware of being dogmatic when dealing with a problem for the solution of which one has to depend on surmise rather than factual data.' Hirst writes: 'As regards the mediaeval and classical plagues, it is quite likely that *P. irritans* did play a subordinate role in the spread of the disease between members of the same household when present in enormous numbers in the bedrooms of cases of septicaemic plague. Only the great numbers could compensate for the intrinsic inferiority of this species as a vector of plague. Yet, even then, there is good reason to believe that *X. cheopis* was present in large numbers in the heavily rat-infested homes of the people and was mainly responsible for the spread of epidemic plague, usually from rat to man, sometimes from man to man. In the light of the experience of the great majority of epidemiologists during the recent pandemic, it seems highly improbable that the human flea could have been the chief agent in the propagation of the major epidemics of the historic period. The belief that *P. irritans* was an import auxiliary in transmitting the infection is most plausible for the period of the Black Death' (p.246). Shrewsbury asserts that *Y. cheopis* was 'almost certainly exclusively responsible for the great mediaeval epidemics of plague in Europe' (p.2.), whilst Biraben writes: '*Pulex irritans* readily transmits the disease... In countries where clothing and inadequate hygiene favour abundant ectoparasites, all human gatherings, urban centres, fairs, armies, processions and so on, can favour the inter-human spread of epidemics', and in an article on the great plague epidemic around Marseilles in 1720-22 he says: 'Numerous factors in the plague epidemic of southern France in 1720-22 can be found which militate in favour of an hypothesis of Ricardo Jorge, who argued that human fleas played an important part in the transmission of plague in western Europe from the Middle Ages until the present.'[3]. This is supported by investigations on rural plague in Iran, Iraq, Syria and Turkey which 'revealed the same complete absence of the rat and the same high density of human ectoparasites.' (W.H.O.Ch).

Whatever the flea, it is pointed out in the literature that not all fleas become infected and only a small proportion of the infected fleas actually transmit the infection. 'Considering the comparative infrequency of such actual vectors of the infection, one must fully agree with the dictum of Webster and Chitre that in the majority of infected fleas, the plague bacillus has entered a blind alley and... one must realise that, though many fleas may be infected, only a minority become infective,' (Pollitzer p.355).

The rat-flea - human-flea controversy has important implications for the historical discussion of plague, some of which will be suggested later in this article, since it involves the possibility of direct transmission of plague from man to man without an intermediate stage involving the rat.

The Spread of Plague

Plague in England has always been part of a great 'pandemic', a widespread outbreak originating in some focus of infection in the Euro-Asian land mass. Recent research distinguishes between:
1. 'Inveterate foci' or 'permanent reservoirs' of plague infection.
2. 'temporary foci' characterised by 'a more or less prolonged persistence following the introduction of plague. This persistence, although suggesting that the disease was permanently implanted. was nevertheless followed by its complete disappearance.'
3. areas characterised by 'the usual brief duration of the historical onslaughts of the disease.'

It is suggested that inveterate foci can only be established where there is a population of very highly resistant sedentary *field rodents* capable of surviving the most violent epizootics in large numbers, together with susceptible rodents able to start epizootic infection afresh. Temporary foci are regarded as due to less resistant and less sedentary field rodents, whilst the brief 'historical' outbreaks are due to epizootics amongst the susceptible commensal rodents such as the black rat. (W.H.O.Ch).

So far as England is concerned, it has certainly never been an inveterate focus, and even the most prolonged outbreak, the Black Death in the fourteenth century, cannot be said with certainty to have provided a temporary focus. Certainly later outbreaks were of 'the usual brief duration.'

There are three aspects of the spread of plague in England, its movement from one settlement to another, from one house to another within a settlement and its spread from one person to another within a single household. Most writers appear to agree that the long-distance spread of plague is not due to the active movement of rats but to the passive transport of fleas on a human body or of rats or fleas in merchandise. Transport in merchandise, is usually regarded as more significant (though one might suppose that this judgement might not hold if the human flea were the predominant vector), and there is disagreement as to the relative importance of transport of fleas and of rats (Hirst pp 320-9, Pollitzer pp 294, 385-391, 490-9). Shrewsbury points out that passive transport would account for the very slow spread of plague from settlement to settlement when transport was slow and for the fact that plague tends to spread along lines of communication. (pp 21-2, 28-9, etc).

An investigation in rural areas of India and Java suggests that there 'plague moved forward step by step, borne by field rodents from field to field, from burrow to burrow, in thin epizootic trails winding across the countryside, infecting village rats in passing, and thus setting off murine epizootics which led in turn to human infection. The sporadic nature of infection in villages, i.e. the fact that in the midst of infected territory many villages remained free from the disease, was due to the capricious nature of these epizootic trails.' (W.H.O.Ch) Whether this happened in England would depend on the existence here at the relevant periods of field rodents capable of carrying the infection in this way, for these rodents vary greatly in their susceptibility.

Transmission from house to house may be by a human carrying an infected flea or by infected rats moving from one house to another. When food is reasonably plentiful the black rat, *R. rattus,* which was the commensal rat in Britain up to the end of the seventeenth century, has a very limited range of movement, and both Shrewsbury and Pollitzer mention the erratic and unpredictable way in which bubonic plague spreads within a settlement. 'Some houses, blocks and even whole precincts being unaffected' (Pollitzer p.300). Again, would this same pattern hold if the ubiquitous human flea were the vector?

What would be the pattern of events within the family? Shrewsbury, committed to the rat-flea theory, proposes a pattern for the intra-familial spread in cases where one member of the family brings in the infection from outside by carrying on his person infected rat fleas. These fleas, deserting their human host for their preferred rat hosts, would engender plague amongst the rats and, after the death of the latter, return to and infect human hosts. He asserts that this would involve an interval of approximately a fortnight between the first death from plague in a family and the second, possibly followed by a number of deaths in a short period, since the infected fleas could now attack the whole family. He describes in detail a number of recorded cases which show this kind of interval (pp. 181,379,424). This might well fit in with an observation by Wu Lien-Teh, reported by Pollitzer (p.485), that in Bombay a rat epizootic (corresponding to an epidemic amongst humans) was followed by an epidemic at an average time-interval of ten to fourteen days, comprising 'three days which, according to laboratory observations, had to elapse before fleas coming from the dead rats were willing to attack man, the average incubation period of human plague (three days) and the average length of illness (five and a half days)'. But it must be noted that the incubation period is reported as varying between one and six days, sometimes even longer, so that one would not expect the Shrewsbury interval to be precise. One might expect that transmission by *P. irritans,* which does not involve going back to the rat, and by *N. fasciatus,* which has a different extrinsic incubation period (Pollitzer p.372) would cause a different intra-familial pattern and it may be that, with the aid of epidemiologists, detailed case studies such as that undertaken here might throw light on this problem. Unfortunately it has not yet been possible to find in the literature any suggested pattern for human-flea infection such as Shrewsbury has proposed for the rat-flea.

The Seasonal Pattern

In bubonic plague, the seasonal pattern is determined by biological factors affecting rats and fleas - their feeding habits, reaction to changes in temperature and humidity and so on. It tends to be a disease of late summer and early autumn, epidemics in Britain reaching a peak around August or September[4]. The degree to which it can persist in cold weather is in dispute, for whilst the outdoor temperature may be too low for flea activity, the indoor temperature may be high enough, and certainly the fleas can survive in the microclimate of the rodents' nests (Hirst p.276, Pollitzer p.258). Shrewsbury tends to be very sceptical of plague deaths in any but very mild winters (pp 159, 163, 224 etc). Again, recent research suggests that in some countries the seasonal nature of plague depends 'primarily on the field rodent factor' (W.H.O.Ch), but there is no way of knowing whether this was true in England.

Although pneumonic plague tends to occur in the colder months of the year, it is by no means confined to them.

Age and Sex Incidence

Most authorities agree that there does not appear to be any difference between the sexes in the incidence of plague. Hirst says that a majority of bubonic cases occurs in persons between ten and thirty-five years of age, the very young and the very old being little affected[5]. Other observers have noted its rarity amongst young children. 'In the experience of most observers', says Pollitzer, 'the incidence of bubonic plague was highest in adolescents and in adults up to the age of forty-five' (p.504). He reports that the incidence of pneumonic plague was highest in the age-group from twenty-one to forty years and that cases among young children and aged persons were rare. (p.516). The prevalent opinion appears to be that these differences are mainly due to varying chances of contact rather than to intrinsic causes. Morris comments that 'pneumonic plague is no respecter of persons and will kill anyone of any age who has inhaled infected droplets' (p.209) and quotes from Stitt's *Tropical Diseases*, 'age, sex and race and occupation are not pre-disposing factors of importance in connection with plague.' This does not, of course, dispose of differences in exposure to infection.

It will be of interest to see whether case-studies of historic plague situations can throw light on this. M.F. and T.H. Hollingsworth, in a study of a London parish in the first quarter of the seventeenth century[6], compared burials in a plague-free period 1600-3 with those in the plague epidemics of 1603 and 1625 and found that the percentage of burials attributed to the age-groups 0-4 and those over 45 decreased in the plague periods, whilst those in the group 5-44 years increased. My own analysis of burials during the plague at Eyam 1665-6 shows a decreased percentage of burials for the age-group 0-5 and increased percentages between 5 and 20 years, with the greatest increase between 10 and 20 years. The Hollings- ✓ N.B. worths found considerably greater mortality amongst men than amongst women, but my study of Eyam shows very little difference between the sexes.

Morris's suggestion that 'some people, doubtless, have a natural or inborn immunity to (bubonic) plague' (p.213) is not borne out by Pollitzer, who writes: 'No convincing evidence is available that a natural immunity to insect-born plague exists in man' (p.133), though Wu Lien-Teh does suggest some natural immunity to pneumonic plague.

The Degree of Mortality caused by Plague

The question of the degree of mortality caused by the major historic plague epidemics, and especially by the Black Death, has long exercised the historians. Whilst the medical literature, strictly speaking, does not throw much light on the subject, it is perhaps reasonable to consider it here.

Estimates made by the historians of mortality in the Black Death vary greatly. J.C. Cox writes, 'from the extant documents of both Church and State it is safe to assume that half the population of England was swept away by plague within a twelve-month'[7],J.C. Russell suggests a quarter.[8] J. Clapham, pointing out that modern experience suggests that some places would remain immune, suggests twenty or twenty-five per cent.[9] G.M. Trevelyan suggests a third or possibly a half,[10] Zinsser a half,[11] whilst William Petty wrote in 1667; 'In pestilential years (which are one in twenty), there dye of ye people 1/6 of ye plague and 1/5 of all diseases', and 'there was never a plague in ye campagne of England by which 1/6 of ye people died',.[12] though Mullet infers that Petty was speaking only of plague in the sixteenth and seventeenth centuries.[13]

An important theme in Shrewsbury's book is that estimates of plague mortality over the country as a whole are almost invariably too high, especially in the Black Death, and he goes so far as to say that "in all probablity the national death roll from 'The Great Pestilence' did not exceed one-twentieth of that population" (p.123). He bases his opinion on three main arguments:

1. that, in the course of a plague epidemic, many deaths were attributed to plague which were, in fact, due to other diseases which did not cease to take their toll during a plague. Indeed, he says, some epidemics were ascribed to plague which were not plague at all. Above all, he is suspicious of serious outbreaks of 'plague' in the winter months.
2. that plague is very uneven in its incidence and is mainly an urban disease. Mortality estimates have relied too heavily on estimates of urban mortality, though some four-fifths of the population lived outside of the large towns and many small towns and country parishes would, in any given epidemic, escape lightly or completely.
3. that the high mortality rates sometimes claimed are contrary to the known nature of bubonic plague.

On the first argument, mistaken attribution, Mullett points out that 'Plague was often a generic word, no more precise than fever or flu. While often indicating bubonic plague, it also covered typhus or even some disorder for which no specific term existed or whose symptoms baffled the observer', and 'Although they recognised the popular tendency to identify the spotted fever with the true plague, the writers believed that ignorance rather than deceit accounted for this practice.'[14] Shrewsbury asserted that 'Typhus fever was not differentiated from bubonic plague until about the middle of the nineteenth century' (pp 125, 141). He quotes a letter from the Mayor of Boston in which, after describing certain symptoms prevalent in the town in 1645, he adds: 'Our physicians seem doubtful whether it were the plague or not, but we for our part are afraid and take it for granted to be plague' (p.414). Morris, on the other hand, asserts: 'After all, plague, at least in its bubonic form, is not difficult to recognise and not very easy to confuse with anything else' (p.210). Yet Pollitzer says: 'The diagnosis of plague must rest upon the results of laboratory examinations rather than on clinical findings, except when well-marked cases are dealt with during fully confirmed outbreaks' (p.446) and 'As noted before, the medical workers in plague areas may be prone to class any patient with enlarged lymph-nodes as suffering from plague' (p.447) and again: 'Generally speaking, the sole presence of general symptoms and signs renders a clinical differentiation of plague from other acute febrile diseases, particularly from pernicious malaria, difficult' (p.447). On the other hand, he also writes: "A clinical prima-facie diagnosis of well-developed 'typical' bubonic plague is easy because, as has been described earlier, the symptoms and signs present in such cases, particularly the manifestations in the primarily affected lymph-nodes, are rather characteristic... However, should doubts exist..." (pp 448-9). McGraith, in *Clinical Tropical Diseases* (1971 edition) says: 'Before the appearance of a bubo, or in primary septicaemic cases, diagnosis may be very difficult to confirm and confusion may arise with typhus.' In the case of pneumonic plague, Wu Lien-Teh indicates that the one acute disease most easily mistaken for pneumonic plague or vice versa is influenza, and that in some countries a differential diagnosis between typhus and plague is difficult. Other diseases which may cause difficulty are, he says, malaria and relapsing fever (pp.278-9). Finally, evidence from physicians of the seventeenth and eighteenth centuries, Thomas Sydenham, writing in the 1660s during a plague epidemic describes the symptoms of a patient and adds 'But whether the fever of which we are now discoursing deserves the name of the plague, I dare not confidently affirm.'[15] Richard Mead, writing in the eighteenth century, when there was no longer plague in England but when interest and anxiety had been aroused by continental epidemics, in a chapter headed 'Of the Signs and Symptoms of Persons Infected with the Plague', gives a clinical description which is by no means specific to plague, whilst in his next chapter, 'Signs upon the Body of an Infected Person', he says that buboes and carbuncles after death 'certainly show any person to be infected with the plague.'[16] The situation appears to be that diagnosis is not difficult where the typical buboes, carbuncles etc. show clearly but, since this is not by means always the case, there is room for difficulty in diagnosis.

On Shrewsbury's second argument we have the following contributions. Mullett writes: 'A most striking characteristic of the Black Death was its uneven incidence and effect. Well-attested calculations have put mortality in some regions very high and in others quite low'[17], though he goes on to say that deaths were still sufficient to dislocate the life of the country. Morris's reply to Shrewsbury is: 'But rats are not unknown in rural areas; and bubonic plague can travel in goods harbouring infected fleas, while pneumonic plague can go to any place whither an infected person carries it. On Shrewsbury's own showing, the highest death rate recorded anywhere was for the remote and scattered Derbyshire village of Eyam in 1665 where five-sixths of the inhabitants died' (p.210). Shrewsbury, in fact, suggests that three-quarters of the inhabitants died, and my own investigation suggests that even this figure is unacceptably high. Moreover, as Shrewsbury points out (p.528), Eyam is not typical, since, at the urging of their clergy, the villagers agreed to a quite unusual degree of segregation which, it is generally agreed, would considerably increase the degree of mortality. Hirst, too, comments on the uneven and irregular distribution of plague in India: 'some areas proving virtually immune to the disease, despite communications with infected zones' (p.105) and Biraben, in the article on the 1720-22 epidemic in southern France quoted above writes: 'On the one hand, a large number of places had a few deaths, sometimes only one: on the other, a large number were severely affected by the plague, losing between twenty and fifty per cent of their populations.'[3] It would appear, then, that it is unwise to base total mortality estimates solely on urban figures or on those for the most severely affected localities.

In his third argument Shrewsbury is concerned with the case-fatality rate of bubonic plague. Statistics from recent plague epidemics, when effective methods of treatment were used, are of little use in considering the historical epidemics, whilst those for the epidemics of the later years of the nineteenth and the earlier years of the twentieth centuries are not very revealing. It is generally recognised that pneumonic and septicaemic plague were then almost invariably fatal, but in respect of bubonic plague we are left with such statements as, from Hirst, 'A substantial proportion of bubonic cases may be expected to recover, even without benefit of those recent discoveries of new methods of treatment... The severity of bubonic cases varies greatly in different epidemics and at different stages of the same epidemic. There is a mild type of plague, known as *pestis minor*, in which the patient is little inconvenienced and may even go about his business, *pestis ambulans.*' (p.30). From Pollitzer we have: 'On the other hand, patients affected by benign forms of bubonic plague without bacteraemia almost invariably recover, even if no treatment is given. The average fatality rate in untreated patients suffering from the usual type of bubonic plague leading to bacteraemia is high, amounting to sixty to ninety per cent in India and China ' (p.418) and from Shrewsbury:'..... modern observations that, in ill-developed countries, urban communities commonly lose about a third of their members from a severe epidemic of bubonic plague' (page 40) and: 'In most of the urban outbreaks in India resulting from the last pandemic which erupted in 1898, about one third of the population was attacked, with a case-mortality rate ranging from seventy to eighty per cent, giving an absolute mortality rate that did not exceed one quarter of the population' (p.49). He emphasises that these are urban rates. It will be recalled that Morris questions Shrewsbury's reliance on the characteristics of bubonic plague and his overlooking of the more deadly pneumonic plague, and this objection has already been discussed in an earlier section.

The Decline of Plague

Two aspects of the decline of plague have received attention; the decline and cessation of a particular epidemic and the disappearance of plague from Britain after 1671 and from western Europe after the first quarter of the following century.

Pollitzer regards an epidemic of bubonic plague in an urban community as self-limiting; that is, its own progress dooms it to decline. It may show a cyclical periodicity with alternate periods of activity and quiescence (Pollitzer p.500, W.H.O. p.10), or, under certain circumstances, it may disappear completely. A number of possible explanations have been suggested but none are conclusively proved.

1. The rat epizootic may cause such mortality amongst the rats that they cease to be sufficiently numerous to maintain the epizootic and, consequently, the epidemic comes to an end (Pollitzer p.492, Hirst p.268, Shrewsbury pp 264, 330). Pollitzer, however, thinks that the importance of this factor is limited, since the erratic spread of the plague epizootic leaves pockets of 'unscathed' rats and the reduced population leads to higher fertility in these pockets (p.492).

2. The rats may gradually acquire resistance to *P. pestis* (Pollitzer p.301, Hirst pp 258,268) Pollitzer points out that there is evidence that this acquired resistance is shortlived and suggests an alternative, that since plague-resistant strains of rat are known to exist, the mortality amongst the non-resistant rats leads to their replacement by the resistant strains, a form of natural selection (Pollitzer pp 132, 301-3, 493, Hirst pp 258, 268). Hirst also hints that: 'it is conceivable that there may even be a change in the reaction of the carrier insect to invasion by the microbe' (p. 259).

3. As with other diseases, the epidemic may stop because there are no longer sufficient persons available to be infected. This may arise through death or flight or by a degree of immunity acquired by those who have caught the disease and recovered from it (Pollitzer pp 137-8, Shrewsbury pp 330, 760).

4. The factor causing the decline may be a reduction in either the infectivity or the pathenogenicity of the bacillus, either in rats or in man or both (Hirst p.259, Shrewsbury p.474). Morris discounts this explanation, saying that 'some experts have doubted whether the virulence of *P. pestis* does significantly vary' (p.212), but the latest World Health Organisation publication on plague, though discussing a rather different point, does suggest the possibility of variation (W.H.O. pp.9-10, 13).

5. Shrewsbury points out that cold weather can be a factor in reducing plague activity (p.264).
Plague may re-emerge after a period of quiescence in a number of ways, notably by the arrival of infected rodents from outside, or by healthy rodents occupying existing burrows in which plague bacilli have lain dormant since the previous epidemic (W.H.O pp.9-10).

Pollitzer remarks that 'rural plague, because it is usually unable to cause a gradual extinction of the susceptible host population, is not a self-limiting disease, but is apt to last for very long periods', but appears to be thinking in terms of 'what might be termed area-wide endemicity, characterised by marked changes in location and extent of the individual out-breaks from season to season' (p.498) so that, for any particular settlement, the effect appears to be much as for urban areas.

It will be noted that the first two of the above explanations are based on the rat-flea theory. Once again, I have not come across equivalent explanations in terms of the human flea.

Wu Lien-Teh believes pneumonic plague to be self-limiting since in passing from lung to lung, *P. pestis* becomes increasingly virulent and leads to 'pulmonary' cases where the lung is affected but does not have pneumonic foci. Such cases are not very infectious since the course of the disease is so rapid that sputum infection is absent and the passing on of the infection declines (p.188).

The disappearance of plague from Britain and western Europe has frequently been attributed to the replacement of the black rat *R. rattus,* by the brown rat, *R. norvegicus.* The theory was that the brown rat is less closely tied to human habitations and that its most common flea, *N. fasciatus,* is a less efficient plague vector (Hirst pp.338-9). But the brown rat has been shown to be responsible for outbreaks in some localities and in any case, so far as Britain is concerned, the extinction of plague took place fifty years before *R. norvegicus* became established in Europe. Pollitzer says no more than that: 'It seems likely that a natural decline of plague was responsible for the cessation of the outbreaks, rather than extrinsic factors which at best could have been of auxiliary importance only and became fully operative well after the disappearance of the evil from Europe' (p.14). Other writers have ascribed the decline to improved hygiene and to the replacement of timber-framed house walls filled with wattle-and-daub by brick and stone building, earth floors by stone, tile or plaster, rushes by carpets, thatched roofs by slates and so on, so that rats ceased to infest human habitations (Hirst p.335). Biraben points out that infection by *Yersinia pseudotuberculosis* conveys complete immunity from plague and speculates that this 'may have been the origin of the disappearance of the great plague epidemics' but he is referring to recent epidemics and points out that *pseudotuberculosis* appeared so recently that it seems unlikely that it could have played a role in the disappearance of plague before the nineteenth century.

Recent writers tend to give the credit to what may be described as public health measures, isolation of patients, quarantine and disinfection. Whilst this appears to be true of the Ottoman Empire in the 1840s, and whilst there are recorded examples of such measures on the Continent in the seventeenth century,[18] there is room for doubt as to whether such measures were effectively applied in England. Petty, writing in 1667, and Mead in 1744 (when there were fears of the re-importation of plague into England from the Continent) suggest such measures in a way which implies that they had not been applied in this country.[19] The debate remains unresolved.

Conclusion

It has not been possible to touch on all the issues in the plague situation which are still unresolved, but enough has been said to show how complex a phenomenon a plague epidemic is and what pitfalls exist for the unwary historian. The degree of mortality caused by the Black Death has been a major issue with historians, and one is left with the impression that Shrewsbury may well be right in his claim that estimates of plague mortality have frequently been too high. But it is not only in the Black Death that the epidemiology of plague impinges upon demographic history. Estimates of plague mortality are equally important, right up to its final disappearance, in the discussion of the relative roles of disease and food shortage in demographic crises.[20] The dispute over whether the rat flea or the human flea was the major vector of bubonic plague has a number of implications which have not yet been fully explored in, for example, the manner and timing of the spread of plague and its winter persistence: and the evidence for one vector as against the other is as yet inadequate. Equally inconclusive is the argument over the disappearance of plague from England and later from the Continent. The date of the cessation is agreed though, as Turner points out in his contribution to this Supplement, the textbooks do not always get it right, but the reason for its cessation has its importance. Does it argue a general improvement in housing and hygiene or merely a decline in the virulence of the bacterium? What has become clear, and here surely the historian owes a debt to Shrewsbury, is that the historical discussion cannot usefully take place without the collaboration of the epidemiologist and that, in a field where the epidemiologists themselves are by no means in complete agreement, the historian needs to proceed with caution.

Notes

1. Extensive quotations are made in this article from the following:
    Plague - R. Pollitzer - World Health Organisation - Geneva 1954.
    A Treatise on Pneumonic Plague - Wu Lien-Teh - World Health Organisation - Geneva 1926
    The Conquest of Plague - L.F. Hirst - Oxford 1953.
    A History of Bubonic Plague in the British Isles - J.F.D. Shrewsbury - Cambridge 1970
    'The Plague in Britain' - C. Morris - A review of Professor Shrewsbury's book in *The Historical Journal* XIV.1. (1971) pp. 205-224.
    'Current Medical and Epidemiological Views on Plague' - A chapter translated from the French of a forthcoming book by Dr. J.N. Biraben.
    W.H.O. Expert Committee on Plague - Fourth Report - W.H.O. Technical Report Series No.447 - Geneva 1970 (this is referred to in this article as 'W.H.O.')
    W.H.O. Chronicle: Vol. 14, No. 11, (1960) pp.419-426. (This is referred to in this article as 'W.H.O.Ch.')
    Pollitzer, Wu Lien-Teh and Hirst are doctors with first hand experience in plague epidemics. Shrewsbury is Emeritus Professor of Bacteriology of the University of Birmingham. Morris is a Cambridge historian and Biraben is Assistant Director of the Institut National d'Etudes Démographiques in Paris.
    Pollitzer and Wu Lien-Teh are difficult for the layman and Shrewsbury is so detailed as to be very laborious to read. Probably the best introductions for the layman are:
    Rats, Lice and History - H. Zinsser - London 1935 and 1943
    The Black Death - P. Ziegler - Collins 1969 and Pelican 1970
    though both appeared before Shrewsbury and cannot take account of his arguments.

2.   *A History of Epidemics in Britain* - Charles Creighton - First Edition Cambridge 1894; second edition Frank Cass 1965.

3.   'Certain Demographic Characteristics of the Plague Epidemic in France' in *Daedalus* (American Academy of Arts and Sciences) Spring 1968.

4.   See, for example, Shrewsbury op. cit. pp. 417,511.

5.   *Brit. Encyc. Med. Pract.* IX. p.676

6.   'Plague Mortality by Age and Sex in the Parish of St. Botolph's without Bishopsgate, London, 1603' - M.F. and T.H. Hollingsworth - in *Population Studies* XXV 1971

7.   *Victoria County History: Hampshire and the Isle of Wight,* Vol. II, p.36.

8.   *British Mediaeval Population* - J.C. Russell - Albuquerque 1948, p.218

9.   *A Concise Economic History of Britain* - J. Clapham - Cambridge 1949, p.117.

10. *English Social History* - G.M. Trevelyan - Longmans Green 1942, p.8.

11. *Rats, Lice and History* - H. Zinsser - London 1935

12. *The Economic Writing of Sir William Petty* - ed. C.H. Hull - Cambridge 1899, p.109

13. *The Bubonic Plague and England* - C.F. Mullett - Univ. of Kentucky Press, pp.254-5.

14. Op.cit. p.258.

15. *The Whole Works of that Excellent Physician Dr. Thomas Sydenham* - ed. John Pechey - London 1734.

16. *A Practical Treatise on the Plague* - Richard Mead - London 1720

17. Op.cit. p.19

18. *Cristofano and the Plague* - C. M. Cipolla - Collins 1973.

19. *The Economic Writing of Sir William Petty* - p. 109
     A Discourse on the Plague - Richard Mead - London 1744

20. See, for example, 'Disease or Famine? Mortality in Cumberland and Westmorland 1580 - 1640' A.B. Appleby - in *Economic History Review,* 2nd Series, XXVI No.3, August 1973.

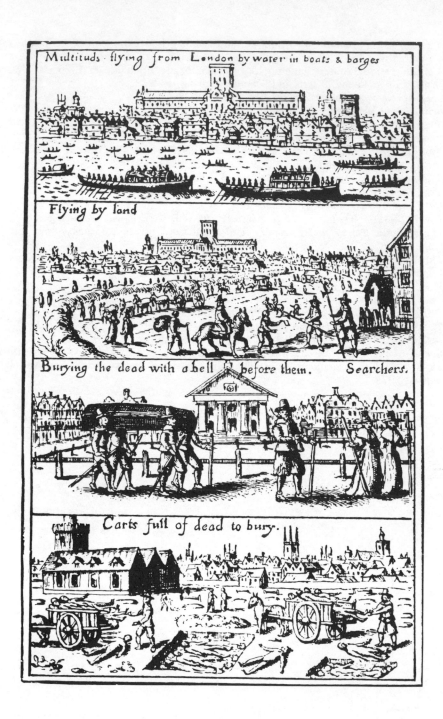

Multituds flying from London by water in boats & barges

Flying by land

Burying the dead with a bell before them.   Searchers.

Carts full of dead to bury.

Current Medical and Epidemiological Views on Plague

Jean-Noel Biraben

Editors' Note

The text of this chapter is taken from Les hommes et la peste, published by Mouton & Co., The Hague, in association with L'Ecole Pratique des Hautes Etudes, Vleme section Paris. We are grateful to the author and the publishers for permission to print this translation by Leslie Bradley and Roger Schofield. The author, Jean-Noel Biraben, is a qualified doctor who works in the National Institute of Demography in Paris. The text contains a number of medical terms which have been translated as such, rather than rendered into everyday speech, so as to preserve the scholarly precision of this valuable summary of the medical and epidemiological characteristics of plague.

A medico-epidemiological introduction would seem to be indispensable for an understanding of the course of historical epidemics of plague.[1] This introduction does not claim to summarise the state of current knowledge of plague; its aim is rather to explain some modern medical and epidemiological ideas which can help to illuminate some important aspects of plague in the past.

The Bacterium

The germ responsible for plague was discovered and described for the first time by Yersin[2] in Hong Kong in 1894. It is a gram-negative coccobacillus from 1 to 1.5 microns in length, showing bipolar staining. It is non-motile, encapsulated and grows in the laboratory on all media at an optimum temperature of 25°C, as an aerobe or faculative anaerobe.

It was formerly included in the genus *Pasteurella*, but both its biochemical and enzymatic properties and its pathogenicity are markedly different, and the genus *Yersinia* was created to mark this distinction. Three main varieties are known to occur in nature. The one most commonly prevalent in ports in the East and in America today is known as *'orientalis'* because it was responsible for the last pandemic which spread from the south of China at the end of the last century. Another variety, at present confined around the Caspian Sea and possibly in Siberia, is called *'mediaevalis'* because it is suspected of having been the origin of the great pandemic which ravaged the whole of the West and the Near East at the time of the Black Death in 1348 and during the following centuries. Finally, a third variety is to be found around the Great Lakes in the Eastern Congo in Africa, which is called *'antiqua'* because it is believed to have been the focus from which the great epidemics of antiquity and the High Middle Ages originated. These three varieties are distinguishable by the presence or absence of certain enzymes, but they are equally pathogenic both to men and to animals.

The plague bacillus carries at least sixteen antigens, certain of which it has in common with the Malassez and Vignal bacillus, or *Yersinia pseudotuberculosis*. The relationship between these two germs is in fact very close, and it is now thought that one can transform itself into the other by a mechanism which remains unknown. The plague bacillus is also very close to a third germ of the same genus, *Yersinia enterocolitica,* which has appeared more recently, but which has spread very rapidly.

Dead plague bacilli filtrates or extracts are toxic to man, but the toxicity varies from one strain to another. Heat, ageing, frequent subculture, and the action of a bacteriophage can reduce the virulence. On the other hand, rapid passage from host to host, involving a very fast selection of the most active strains, gives the illusion of an increasing virulence. The plague bacillus is capable of penetrating into the human organism through the mucous membranes but not it seems through healthy skin, though it must be understood that very minute excoriations, for example those caused by shaving or depilation, are enough to permit penetration.

It was long believed that certain germs (streptococci, pneumococci etc.) exhibited an action hostile to the plague bacillus, that is to say their development arrested that of *Yersinia pestis*. This phenomenon is real enough 'in vitro', but it appears that observations on this subject made 'in vivo' may perhaps be another example of an illusory effect. For the disappearance of the plague bacillus probably precedes the second infection, and this would make the latter only an epiphenomenon, rather than the cause, of the disappearance. This second infection is extremely rare today, although formerly it was very frequent; indeed barber-surgeons even used to try to provoke it because they saw in it a sign favourable to their patients' recovery.

Although naturally occurring strains of *Yersinia pestis* are never found to be infected with bacteriophages, phages capable of lysing them have been observed in the filtrates of sewage water and even in human stools.

Finally, the plague bacillus can survive for only a few days in putrifying corpses, but survival can extend to several years if the corpses remain frozen. Similarly, the bacillus disappears rapidly from surface soil; but it can survive for months and sometimes even for years if kept in the dark and at a constant temperature, as in a sealed test tube in a laboratory, or underground, particularly in the microclimate of rodents' burrows.

The Disease

In man the plague bacillus has a very marked toxic action. It produces cell necrosis and provokes generalised inflammatory reactions, more specifically in the nervous tissues. It is readily phagocytosed but resists being lysed by polymorphs and continues to multiply in them, thereby becoming disseminated throughout the whole body. Accumulations of the bacillus obstruct the dilated capillaries, leading to haemorrhagic suffusions, and in the capsules of the enlarged lymph nodes it infiltrates the nerve fibres, for which it has an especial affinity, with a blood-tinged oedema. It seems that this distension and infiltration by bacilli are responsible for the terrible pain of bubonic plague.

Clinically two forms are distinguished, differing essentially in the way the bacterium enters the organism. Generally speaking this can be either through the skin or through the lungs.

In the bubonic form, following skin penetration, the incubation period is from one to six days.

In a number of very rare cases the disease can assume a mild ambulatory form which manifests itself as a simple swelling of the lymph nodes lasting from one to three weeks and beginning with some minor generalised symptoms: a mild increase in temperature, headaches, vague pains.[3]

In the normal case a very acute onset is observed with a temperature of 39 or 40°C. The point of inoculation is almost always a flea-bite on a limb. Here a pustule or plague blister forms, which rapidly necroses then forms a gangrenous blackish plaque called a plague carbuncle. Although it is very generally observed, this carbuncle does not appear in some epidemics and so is not an absolutely invariable symptom. Then, from the second or third day, there is an enlargement of the lymph nodes, usually in the groin but sometimes in the armpit or the neck, draining the site of infection.[4] The lymph nodes become large, hard, very painful and tend to suppurate. These are the buboes.

In addition to a high temperature, generalised symptoms are more or less pronounced, but neurological and psychological disturbances are also frequent: headaches and clouding of the faculties are often the first symptoms felt by the patient. Until about 1880 authors almost always report intestinal disturbances, such as vomiting and sometimes diarrhoea, but these symptoms are now very rare, possibly due to changes in diet. At the end of eight or ten days the disease may suddenly terminate and convalescence begin. Varying from epidemic to epidemic between 20 per cent and 40 per cent of those infected survive. Otherwise an acute septicaemic stage sets in with multiple visceral involvement of the heart, kidneys and lungs; the temperature rises to 40 or 42°C and death can supervene at this point. If death is delayed, subcutaneous embolic lesions can be seen to form new pustules which necrose and turn gangrenous, forming new carbuncles. Spontaneous haemorrhages of the mucous membranes and the viscera multiply, with purpura, haematuria and large subcutaneous spots which, like ecchymoses, variously change colour between orange and black, blue, mauve and yellow. Historically these haemorrhagic forms with spots appear to have been more frequent than they are today, and they made a great impression on contemporary observers. Next the neurological and psychological disturbances rapidly become more acute (vertigo and hallucinations accompanied by delirium, or more rarely somnolence), and end very suddenly in coma and death.

Some writers have used the term 'septicaemic' for cases which lead to death in twenty-four to thirty-six hours. After an extremely severe onset, the patient suddenly falls into an immobile state, with a temperature of 40 - 42°C, and dies without any bubo being visible and at the most after occasionally having suffered haemorrhages. In this case, which is relatively common especially at the beginning of an epidemic, either the bubo has not had time to develop or the lymph node concerned is too deep to be seen at this stage, as is the case, for example, with the mesenteric nodes. But it is still of the bubonic type, as are the extreme cases of sudden death, which are far from exceptional, being frequently reported by authors in all periods.

In outbreaks of bubonic plague in late nineteenth century Europe, fatalities occurred on average as follows: 1 per cent to 2 per cent died suddenly, 30 to 40 per cent before the second day after being attacked, 50 to 55 per cent before the eighth day, 60 to 65 per cent before three weeks, 80 to 90 per cent before the fourth week and the others later. The first and third weeks were therefore the most lethal. Time of recovery was just as variable. Half of those who survived recovered at the end of six to eight days, almost all the others between two and five weeks, although some took two or three months to recover because of suppuration of the bubo.

A frequency distribution of the clinical forms of the disease is shown in the following table which is based on 61 cases documented at Porto in 1899.[5]

30 deaths:	3	'fulminant'
	12	rapid: from a few hours to four days
	8	simple bubonic
	2	haemorrhagic (external haemorrhages, haematuria)
	2	'exanthematic' (subcutaneous or internal petechiae and ecchymoses)
	3	secondary pneumonic
31 recoveries:	27	simple bubonic
	1	haemorrhagic
	3	secondary pneumonic

In historical epidemics of bubonic plague it is frequently found that in a certain number of cases a plague abscess in the lungs ruptures. Since the patient coughs, bacteria can be transmitted through inhalation and via the mucous membranes. Climatic conditions play an important role, to which we will return when we study the epidemiology, but plague contracted in this way has very different clinical features. This is pneumonic plague.

In the primary pneumonic form the incubation period is only from one to three days. The onset is very severe, with a temperature of only 38°C, but the pulse reaches 120 per minute. The patient feels a retrosternal constriction and a stitch in the side, then he coughs, gently at first with some sputum, then more violently with bloodstained sputum. Then difficulty in breathing makes him anxious; soon he has to sit down to breathe and he coughs more and more, expectorating sputum which is frothy and tinged with blood. Finally, this progressive and distressing asphyxia and cyanosis is followed by neurological difficulties such as motor inco-ordination, then coma, and in every case death occurs within two or three days.

Plague bacillus, when innoculated, is pathogenic for the majority of mammals, especially rodents. In man there is no natural immunity, but though his susceptibility is always very high, the virulence of the bacillus itself can vary in the course of an epidemic. Frequently strains are isolated at the end of an epidemic which are less virulent than those at the beginning, and this poses a problem which has not yet been solved.

On the other hand, after recovery, which is often accompanied by after effects[6], a certain acquired immunity can be observed, which lasts from some months to several years depending on the individual case. Vaccination with killed bacilli only provides a brief immunity, but Girard's live vaccine gives protection for several years.

Modern treatment is based on antibiotic therapy. Streptomycin is most often used and is very effective, as is tetracycline. Sulphonamide therapy gives good results: sulphathiazole is an excellent prophylactic, sulphamerazine and other products in the same group have some activity, but are not powerful enough to be effective in pneumonic plague. The success of therapy with antisera is poor and it is rarely used.

Epidemiology

Methods of Infection

Infection by bubonic plague remained a mystery for a long time until it was discovered by Simond at Bombay in 1898; it occurs through a vector, the flea, which inoculates the disease by biting its host. According to the classical mechanism a plug of bacilli and blood blocks the proventriculus of the infected flea, a sort of small pouch situated on the oesophagus. When the flea bites, the blood which it has sucked in rebounds on this plug and, being unable to pass, is regurgitated infected back into the wound. But fleas without a proventriculus can also transmit the disease, for contamination can occur not only through biting but also through the excrement of an infected flea touching excoriations of the skin such as scratches, or even quite independently of the flea through the ingestion of infected substances, as when hunters eat infected game. Finally and more rarely, but not so exceptionally as was formerly thought, transmission can be effected by lice and even bugs.

The nature of the infective power of the flea is complex and varies from one strain to another even in the same species. Even when suffering from inanition an infected flea can survive for several months, and even for a year in certain very favourable conditions. It can then constitute a reservoir of bacilli, whether it survives in a rodent's fur, or in dust on the ground and on floors. The part it can play was shown, for example, in the persistence of plague in Madagascar, where infected fleas could be found in the dust of the beaten earth floors of the houses.

One should emphasise that the different species of flea have a marked specificity for a given host, except temporarily in the very rare cases where they cannot find their normal host. The cat flea lives only on the cat, the dog flea on the dog and so on. There are only a few exceptions to this rule, but they are of great importance for our subject. In practice *Coratophylus fasciatus* lives indifferently on wild and domestic rats and so ensures the transmission of plague from one to the other, and *Xenopsylla cheopis,* which lives on domestic rats can, in the absence of rats, bite man. [7] It is this latter flea which is responsible for passing plague from rat to man, and for a long time it was thought that it alone was responsible for all epidemics, both because it plays an important role in modern epidemics, and because the human flea, *Pulex irritans,* has no proventriculus. But *Pulex irritans,* which lives only on man, readily transmits the disease and its importance depends on the number of humans infected.

In very dry tropical countries, where people live almost entirely naked and where baths are frequently taken, human fleas are rare and plague is reduced to some sporadic cases arising from *Xenopsylla* which have abandoned dead rats. On the other hand in countries where clothing and inadequate hygiene favour abundant human infestation, all human gatherings (urban centres, fairs, armies, processions etc.) can favour the spread of epidemic directly from man to man.

In order to survive the flea needs very rigid conditions of temperature and humidity; it does well at 15° to $20^{\circ}C$ with 90 to 95 per cent humidity, for example in clothing on the body. Cold limits its activity and heat retards its reproduction, but neither has any effect on its longevity, which is controlled by humidity. At $20^{\circ}C$ the flea dies if the humidity falls to 70 per cent, and it survives only seven to eight days at 80 per cent. Its susceptibility to changes in humidity increases with temperature. Thus in natural conditions its longevity varies from two days to a year; its activity is low in winter and very important in summer.

The flea lays its eggs in the dust or in crevices in floors, but the eggs only survive and subsequently hatch if temperature and above all humidity are suitable. Thus in moderate conditions they can survive weeks and sometimes even two to three months until rainfall makes them all hatch at once.

Curiously, the flea is very attracted to white objects, and it is found for preference on white fabrics, bedclothes or clothing. On the other hand it is repelled by the smell of certain animals (horses, cows, sheep, goats and camels which, although readily susceptible to plague, rarely contract it because they have no fleas), as well as by the smell of certain food oils (olive oil, nuts, peanuts). These peculiarities, mere curiosities today, were widely recognised empirically by many societies in the Middle Ages and the Renaissance, and were used as means of avoiding infection.

While the flea (or the louse) transmits plague in its bubonic form, pneumonic plague is communicated from man to man, usually by droplets of saliva emitted while speaking or coughing. These droplets, called Flügge droplets, are projected a distance of about two metres in normal speech, and three or four metres in coughing or sneezing. In cold, damp countries they remain infective for a long time and can be inhaled so long as they are in suspension in the atmosphere. The bacillus then enters the body through the mucosa of the nose, mouth or lung. The same process can occur when infected animals are dismembered or when objects soiled by spittle are handled and the fingers later touch the mucosa (mouth, eyes, nose) for dried spittle in a cold country remains infective for a long time.

Pneumonic plague is thus essentially associated with cold countries or with winter in temperate countries.[8] In all other situations it is unusual or very limited in extent, although it is worth remembering that its high degree of inter-human infectivity and its 100% death rate make it an extremely dangerous form of plague.

Reservoirs of the bacteria.

The rat has long been considered to be the sole origin of plague epidemics, and in 1894 Roux and Yersin had no hesitation in writing; 'Plague is a disease of the rat, incidentally transmitted to man.' It was only around 1925 that Ricardo Jorge introduced the idea of sylvatic plague, throwing into relief the role of wild rodents, which in fact can maintain permanent foci of plague. There are several examples: the Tarbagan, a species of large marmot in Central Asia near Lake Baikal; the spermophili or susliks in southeast Russia; the meriones, 60 per cent of whose fleas are *Xenopsyllae,* in the Near East, Iran and Turkestan; the ground squirrels or *Citellus beecheyi* in North America; the Cuis or wild guineapigs in South America; probably rats near Lake Alberta and a mouse *Mastomys coucha* round Lake Kivou in Central Africa; gerbils in South Africa etc.[9]

Analysis of the permanent plague foci in the Near East has provided a partial solution to the problem of their persistence. It is now known that the germs survive for a long time in the earth of the burrows of meriones, where the microclimate is favourable, and infect rodents from neighbouring areas, which in the course of time come to occupy those burrows whose former tenants are dead. But it is also known that the meriones' resistance to plague largely depends on the method of infection. They tolerate plague fairly well if it is inoculated under the skin, for example by a flea, but die if they contract a pulmonary plague through burrowing in an infected burrow.

In the Indies today plague persists through a related process. The activity of field rodents spreads it from burrow to burrow in a random manner, infecting the village rats on the way and thereby starting a murine epizootic which leads to human infection, although some villages are left unscathed in the midst of the general infection. It is highly seasonal, being subject to the ecological cycle of the rodents and the biology of the fleas. At the end of May the field rodents start to aestivate, digging out their galleries and living on reserves accumulated in their burrows. From this time the plague ceases to spread; it stops in the villages where it had been raging for months, and soon afterwards dies out in the villages which were last to be affected, although on very rare occasions the murine epizootic allows the infection to carry over from one season to the next. When the rains cease in mid-October and the wild rodents emerge and invade the empty but infected burrows, the epizootic starts again followed by murine plague and then human plague.

There is another rarer, though well researched, way in which the disease can persist. Hibernating wild rodents having contracted plague can suffer an inconspicuous subclinical infection throughout the whole period of hibernation. When they awake the infection suddenly becomes active again and the disease kills them off. This is the case with the Tarbagans of the region of Lake Baikal, for example, and Dujardin-Beaumetz has reproduced the same phenomenon with alpine marmots.

In addition to these permanent sylvatic foci there are temporary centres in certain big towns and above all in ports, where nowadays two species of domestic rat can be found. The first species, the Black Rat *(Rattus rattus),* is fairly delicate, its tail is longer than its body and the colour of its fur differs according to the variety,[10] It has been established in Europe at least since the late Middle Ages, but it is not known whether it was present in antiquity and in the early middle ages.[11] It is very sedentary, it has never been found more than 200 metres from a habitation, and it likes dry places. Above all it lives in attics and on ships, of which it is

31

a habitual tenant. If it travels it is always as a passive passenger from one village to another or from one port to another. It is this rat which has been responsible for infecting man in Europe in the past.

The second species, the Grey or Brown Rat *(Rattus norvegicus)*, originated in eastern and central Asia and only became widespread in Europe at the end of the eighteenth century, and in the Mediterranean basin at the beginning of the nineteenth century.[12] It has a shorter tail, and it is larger and more robust than the Black Rat, which it supplants when they meet. It is less tied to man and generally lives in cellars and sewers, for it swims very well and loves a humid atmosphere. It is very rare on ships. Occasionally it travels across fields, and rural colonies have been observed in burrows near hedgerows or on the banks of streams, sometimes more than 600 metres from a village.

Rats attain sexual maturity at the age of four months. The females only accept mating when they are in rut. They have about four litters a year, each on average comprising six young. Rats are very active, but only at night, and are hostile to others who intrude on the territory of their clan. They are individualists and never take part in concerted action in groups, but they recognise a hierarchy. They make their nests, sleep and eat only in sheltered places, and behave (especially *norvegicus*) like inquisitive explorers, distrustful of the world outside their territory.[13]

Rattus norvegicus would appear to be rather less susceptible to plague than the Black Rat. The latter would introduce the germ when arriving by ship, the former would then contract the disease and spread it throughout the rat population. The fleas of the two species, the *Xenopsylla,* would occasionally bite man and so constitute a reservoir of the bacillus leading eventually to an outbreak of plague several years later.

Yersinia Pseudotuberculosis

This bacillus, discovered in 1893 by Malassez and Vignal in a guineapig in Paris, is a near relative of the plague bacillus, from which it could have originated or which it could produce by some still undiscovered process. It is similar in appearance but differs in motility.

It is only since the school of Tübingen drew attention to it in 1954 that it has been carefully studied and become better known through several published papers.

It is relatively innocuous to man: the first reported human case was diagnosed by Albrecht in Germany in 1910. It particularly affects children, in whom it produces an adenitis, usually of the mesenteric lymph nodes with medullary and especially cortical micro-abscesses, together with fever and abdominal pain. The ganglia are sometimes palpable in the right iliac fossa and they are painful on pressure, but silent attacks are much more frequent, especially in adults and particularly females. In a girls' boarding school in the northwest of France an epidemic which lasted from September 1965 to March 1966 showed that out of 64 persons 44 were attacked, but only 7 presented clinical symptoms.[14]

The disease is very mild amongst children, in whom it is sometimes taken for appendicitis, and recovery follows spontaneously in a few days. Sometimes, especially between 8 and 15 years of age, the intestinal infection is followed immediately by an erythema of the joints, and this type has become sufficiently frequent to represent more than half of all known cases of erythema of the joints in France today. In adults over 30 years of age the disease is much rarer, but it can be serious and there are even reports of some septicaemic cases proving fatal.[15]

The infection does not seem to cause any disease in rats and mice; the animal merely becomes a life-long carrier of the germ. Other rodents like the hare, which is the European animal most affected, and the rabbit are very susceptible and often catch it in a fatal septicaemic form. Many other animals are also very susceptible, for example the roe deer, the monkey, particularly the cat which is often a source of infection for man, and birds like turkeys, chickens, pheasants, partridges etc.[16] Pigeons, on the other hand, are more resistant, and like rats appear to act as carriers of the germ. The flea too can eventually transmit it.

In man as in animals the bacilli are excreted in the stools and infection almost always arises from polluted food, for example raw vegetables fertilised with human manure, since the bacillus survives quite well in the soil.

It is of considerable interest that even in the absence of clinical symptoms the disease gives both man and the rat 100 per cent immunity against the plague bacillus.[17] The hypothesis may therefore be advanced that the appearance of this new disease may have been the origin of the disappearance of the great plague epidemics. Though too many unknowns still surround the question of when and where it first appeared for any definite conclusions to be drawn, it seems very probable that its diffusion is extremely recent. For example though it has been known in France and Germany since the end of the nineteenth century, it only appeared in Tunisia in 1927, and then crossed Algeria to reach Morocco only in 1943. It is still unknown in Turkey, in the Lebanon and in Israel. In Russia it covers almost all the European republics, and Russian scientists now follow its annual progress along the lower Volga and to the north of the Caspian Sea in the direction of Turkestan. It has also spread through the trade in live animals for breeding but in a completely random way, being introduced through the ports very early in some countries (for example in Japan since 1910, in Dakar in 1933), but very late in others (at Vladivostock in 1959, in South Africa in 1960, in Canada and New Zealand in 1963).

Given these conditions, if we consider the ravages wrought by plague in Western Europe up to the eighteenth century and in Eastern Europe up to the nineteenth century, it seems unlikely, though one can never be certain, that pseudotuberculosis could have played a role in the disappearance of plague either in Antiquity or in the High Middle Ages. It is even doubtful, or at least very debatable, whether pseudotuberculosis was significant in these same areas in the nineteenth century.

As for the future of these diseases, it would be presumptious to assert that their fate is settled. Sylvatic plague is today more widespread in the world than it has ever been, and the virulence of its germ to man has not weakened at all. Within a few decades the international trade in animals will spread pseudotuberculosis over the greater part of the earth's surface, driving plague into areas and onto species which it cannot reach and upsetting biological equilibria everywhere. Finally, either plague or pseudotuberculosis may undergo chance mutations and produce new forms unforseeable in the present state of our knowledge.

Yersinia Enterocolitica

Discovered in 1923 at New York by Schleifstein and Coleman in a patient with a suppurating dermatitis of the chin with cervical lymphadenopathy, this bacillus presents great analogies with *Yersinia pseudotuberculosis,* especially in its laboratory characteristics. However it displays no cross-immunity with the other *Yersinia,* and too little is still known of it for us to know whether it can originate from these germs or produce them by mutation.

Rediscovered in 1932 in the United States and in Copenhagen, it was again lost to view until 1948. Since 1954 its frequency in man as well as in animals has been growing and spreading rapidly.

Clinically it produces in man enterocolitis with diarrhoea and sometimes abdominal pains, vomiting and a steady high temperature, which can rise to 39°C in two thirds of cases.[18] Yet the disorder can assume the most varied forms ranging from the healthy carrier and a mild twentyfour-hour diarrhoea to fatal septicaemia, and passing through every anatomical localisation: erythema of the joints (especially in women under the age of twenty), ulcerative dermatitis or pyodermatitis, arthritis (mainly of the knees), osteitis, conjunctivitis and even retinal haemorrhage, abscess of the spleen, the liver, the lining of the stomach, etc. It is a disease which is rare in summer and common in winter. Though all ages are susceptible and both sexes are equally affected[19], out of more than 1,000 human cases published since 1964 about one third related to children of less than two years[20]. But though recovery in fifteen days to two months accompanied by the disappearance of the germ at the time of a follow up examination is often, although not invariably, the case, individuals with physiological impairments (through age, cirrhosis, diabetes mellitus haemopathy or even a transfusion or treatment by immunosuppressors) often develop a septicaemia which is fatal in one case out of two in spite of early treatment.

The disease is also very varied in its symptoms in numerous wild animals like the hare, or in breeding animals like the chinchilla, or even in domestic animals like the dog and the pig. The fact that the enterocolitica strains of the latter are identical with certain strains found in man gives rise to the suspicion that the infection may be mainly of an alimentary origin, though it has not yet been possible to produce it either in this way or in any other experimental situation.

The interest of this bacillus for the subject of plague lies above all in its extreme instability. Indeed its biochemical, serological and lysotypical properties suggest that we are dealing with a very recent germ, still too recent to offer a clear ecological resolution, and this in turn suggests that the resources of the genus *Yersinia* are far from being exhausted.[21]

Notes

1. I am very grateful to Professor Henri H. Mollaret for his unstinted help and advice, and for patiently answering all my questions. I am also indebted to Madame Jacqueline Brossollet who has allowed me unrestricted access to the rich collection of documents held by the Department of Plague at the Institut Pasteur.

2. Kitasato, who thought that he had discovered the plague bacillus, acknowledged his mistake at the Congress of Medicine of the Far East over which he presided in 1925, thereby giving an example of the highest scientific probity. See Henri Jacotot: 'Dr. Alexander Yersin', *Bulletin de la Société des Etudes Indochinoises,* 1er trimestre 1944, pp. 23-25.

3. As we shall see this form is especially conspicuous in the last stages of an epidemic when it is in decline.

4. In the outbreak of plague in Porto in 1899, out of 103 instances of buboes the following distribution was observed: groin nodes 25, crural 23, axillary 14, cervical 12, retromaxillary 11, pectoral 3, other sites 15. J. Ferran, Vinas et Grau, *La peste bubonicia,* Barcelona 1907.

5. *Ibid.,* p. 209. It is noteworthy that just over half of the dossiers concern patients who recovered. This proportion reflects not only the degree of effectiveness of modern treatment, but also the fact that sudden deaths at home were more likely to have been omitted from the medical records.

6. After—effects are unknown today, but were common in historical times doubtless owing to the treatments used. Neurological symptoms were often observed, especially tics, spasmodic contractions etc. And above all, especially in the period up to the 17th century, there were cutaneous lesions in the region of the bubo, sometimes forming huge scars with a keloid formation, perhaps because of the cauterising of the bubo with a hot iron.

7. It is the same with the mouse flea, *Leptopsylla musculi,* which cannot transmit plague from mouse to mouse but occasionally bites domestic rats, although never man. Sometimes however, as in Madagascar, mice have *Xenopsylla cheopis* as parasites.

8. Thus in Madagascar it sometimes occurs on the High Plateau, never on the low warm coastlands.

9. In addition to the domestic rat, the main wild rodents susceptible to plague in France are the vole, the dormouse, the Alsatian hamster and the alpine marmot. But they are incapable of maintaining a permanent focus of plague, doubtless because they are too susceptible to it.

10. The variety known as Alexander's Rat has a browny-red fur.

11. Hirst has argued that rats have been known in Europe since the Pleistocene era, but the question remains unresolved. L.F. Hirst, *The Conquest of Plague,* Oxford University Press 1953, pp. 122—6. For an excellent summary of the palaeontology and history of the different species of rat see J.F.D. Shrewsbury, *A History of Bubonic Plague in the British Isles,* Cambridge University Press 1970, pp. 7—16.

12. It was recorded for the first time at Copenhagen in 1716 having been introduced by Russian ships. It reached England in 1728, Germany in 1750, Paris in 1753, Norway in 1762, Spain in 1800 and Switzerland in 1809. International trade spread it from Europe to the east coast of the U.S.A. in 1775 and it gradually spread to reach Wyoming in 1919 and Montana in 1923. The same pattern is repeated in the great ports of Brazil, Madagascar and Australia.

13. S.A. Barnett, 'Rats', *Scientific American* (January 1967), p. 79–85, reports a census of rats carried out in 1948 and 1949 in two English villages where rat catching was little practised. The numbers were estimated on the basis of the amount of food consumed daily, which is about the equivalent of 24 grammes of grain per rat. Each village contained 15 or so nests with 12 to 20 rats each located near the most important sources of food.

	Inhabitants	Cats	Dogs	Rats
Village 1	364	55	25	330
Village 2	266	43	14	180

14. H.H. Mollaret, J. Brunet and R. Gurne, 'Une nouvelle épidémie due au bacille de Mallasez et Vignal', *Le Concours Médical,* 3 Décembre 1966.

15. Note that 'in vivo' tetracycline considerably increases the virulence of the Malassez and Vignal bacillus; a single dose administered to a guineapig, which until then has been a healthy carrier, is enough to unleash an overwhelming septicaemia which kills the animal in two to three days.

16. Birds are not susceptible to plague and cannot carry *Yersinia pestis.*

17. Research by Schutz in 1922. In 1932 Colonel Boyer tried to use this property to check a plague epidemic in Madagascar, but it is extremely difficult to reproduce pseudo-tubercular disease under experimental conditions.

18. Only stool culture and serology enable *Yersinia enterocolitica* to be differentiated; the clinical picture, terminal ileitis and mesenteric adenitis being similar to the effects of *pseudotuberculosis* or even to those of *Salmonella* or *Shigella.*

19. In the literature extreme ages of seven months and eightyfive years are reported.

20. H.H. Mollaret, 'L' infection humaine à *Yersinia enterocolitica* en 1970 à la lumière de 624 cas récents, aspects cliniques et perspectives épidémiologiques', *Pathologie-Biologie,* (February 1971). Between the writing of this article on the first of September 1970 and its printing on January 21st 1971, 138 new human cases were registered at the Centre National des Yersinia at the Institut Pasteur.

21. Outside the United States and Denmark, which have already been mentioned, its first appearance in different countries was as follows: Switzerland in 1948, England in 1953, France in 1958 (where it is only known north of the line drawn between St. Malo and Geneva) Algeria in 1959, Canada in 1960, Federal Germany in 1962, Sweden and the Netherlands in 1963, Belgium in 1964 (this is the country where the human variety is the most common; Belgium accounts for 350 out of 1,000 published cases), Finland in 1965, South Africa in 1966, Czechoslovakia, U.S.S.R., Norway and the Cameroons in 1967, Rumania, Brazil and the Congo Kinshasa in 1968, Hungary in 1969.

Plague in Britain

Christopher Morris

This is a review of 'A History of Bubonic Plague in the British Isles' by J.F.D.Shrewsbury, Cambridge University Press, 1970. It first appeared in 'The Historical Journal' and we are grateful to the Journal's editors and to the Cambridge University Press for permission to reprint it.

Historians of many kinds, perhaps economic historians and demographers most of all, will be grateful to Professor Shrewsbury for the enormous labours which have gone into this all but definitive history of plague in Britain. He has ransacked virtually all published local histories and parish records and he has read very widely in contemporary chronicles and memoirs. He has also shrewdly drawn attention to areas where more research still needs to be done. He has, moreover, exploded a certain number of myths and old wives' tales, even if at times he has warmed to this work a little over-zealously. In places he has something distinctly original to say — particularly on the geographical incidence of plague. His book is also embellished with numerous illuminating maps, graphs and tables.

Perhaps Professor Shrewsbury's most arresting and most convincing hypothesis is that the Great Plague of London (1665) may only have been, in proportion to London's population, the third most destructive of the city's last five great outbreaks (1563, 1593, 1603, 1625, 1665). In other words, 'the Great Plague' is thought great only because it was the last and because its aggregate toll is the highest. Shrewsbury awards the prize for proportional destruction to the plague of 1563 and his grounds for doing so are reasonably sound. But it should be noted that, in each case, he takes only the official figures, drawn from the mortality bills, which he himself admits to be almost certainly an underestimate in the case of 1665. The official figure for that year is 68,596; and Shrewsbury accepts Bell's view that the real number may well have exceeded 100,000.[1] But the same doubts may be applicable to the official figures given for the four earlier epidemics. We know that in the worst weeks of an outbreak it became virtually impossible to keep proper records, that there was much faulty diagnosis and much deliberate concealment,[2] and that the records cannot include fugitives who fled with the infection already in them and died outside the city. Some parishes, too, were self-evidently dishonest, as Shrewsbury admits, though he does not draw attention to the strange coincidence by which the parish clerk of St. Giles', Cripplegate, and his wife both died allegedly of 'dropsy' on the same day in the worst plague week of 1665.[3] Nor are we told that, in the official figures, the 28,710 Londoners who died in 1665 supposedly of something other than plague come to over twice the average annual mortality in London from all causes for the previous five years. Similar suspicions ought, surely, to arise before we accept the official figures for the earlier outbreaks.

Nevertheless, Shrewsbury is certainly at his best on 1665, partly because here, with due acknowledgement, he can lean heavily on Bell's excellent book. Elsewhere, however, he displays certain limitations and some curious blind spots. Since this is the kind of book whose conclusions, if unchallenged, could easily become an orthodoxy overnight, it is necessary to draw attention to numerous questions which the author appears to have begged. Nearly all of them arise from one cause. Professor Shrewsbury's labours, oddly enough, have been labours more of hate than of love. He is out, whenever he can, to play down the plague, to prove that many deaths attributed to it were in fact due to something else and that its destructiveness, particularly in the Great Pestilence of 1348–50, has been enormously exaggerated. Shrewsbury is an Emeritus Professor of bacteriology but, paradoxically, more of his blind spots seem due to questionable views on the behaviour of the disease than to any serious deficiencies in his historical scholarship.

At this point, for the benefit of the uninitiated, it is necessary to summarize the basic medical facts which are somewhat complex.

The causative agent of plague is *Pasteurella pestis,* a non-motile bacillus needing a vector to convey it to a victim. In 'nature' so to speak, plague is a disease of wild rodents, especially of rats. Both species of the rat, *Rattus norvegicus* (the brown rat) and *Rattus rattus* (the black rat) are susceptible, the brown one being liable to get the disease first but, for reasons which will appear later, being slightly less dangerous to man. Afflicted rats suffer from severe bacteraemia; that is, they have innumerable bacilli in their blood stream. From this their fleas ingest the bacilli which then form a kind of culture blocking the flea's oesophagus and preventing efficient swallowing. The flea itself does not get the disease but it does become very hungry and, when the rat dies and grows cold, the flea may bite any available human or other animals. As it bites the flea regurgitates bacilli into the victim's blood; and infection can also occur through the entry of the flea's faeces into the bite. If a man is bitten he will develop a bubo or painful swelling in the lymphatic glands which drain the infected limb—in the groin if the bite is on the leg, in the armpit if he is bitten on the arm, or in the neck if bitten on the face. The plague toxins may give rise to high fever, coma, heart failure, inflammation of the spleen or kidneys and sometimes destruction of tissue and consequent internal haemorrhage. The mortality rate in bubonic cases untreated by modern drugs ranges between 60 and 85 per cent, and death on the average occurs after five days of illness.

For reasons which are still not clear the disease may occasionally set up general blood-poisoning, septicaemic plague, which is invariably fatal and may kill within a day; and in septicaemic cases the human flea (*Pulex irritans*) can easily become the vector. More important, plague can produce a secondary pneumonia (again, for reasons not yet known) and from this an epidemic of pneumonic plague may arise—although in some conditions the disease may take a primary pneumonic form from the outset. In pneumonic cases the mortality rate is at least 99.99 per cent and the patient dies in three days or even less.

Bubonic plague is spread normally by the rat flea alone (principally *Xenopsylla cheopis*), which will bite man readily if rodents are not available. As a rule then bubonic plague depends exclusively on flea-bite. If infected rodents or their blocked fleas are not present there can be no epidemic. But a rodent migration is not necessarily required for the spread of plague since infected fleas, and occasionally infected rats, can travel long distances in grain, clothing or other merchandise. Moreover, a blocked flea, in favourable conditions, can remain alive and infectious for up to fifty days even without food.[4] The flea usually hibernates in winter and therefore, in temperate climates, the height of the bubonic season is the summer.

The case is vastly different with pneumonic plague, which is spread by droplet infection, through coughing or sneezing, from man to man and is in fact the most dangerous of all diseases to nurse, with the possible exception of smallpox. It is also invariably accompanied by the expectoration of bloody sputum. It flourishes in cold weather or cold climates, partly because people are more liable to be in close proximity indoors. There is also some evidence that when plague is invading virgin territory it is apt to appear in its pneumonic form, and also when it originates from burrowing rodents such as marmots, tarbagans, susliks, ground-squirrels or prairie dogs.[5]

Professor Shrewsbury of course knows all these facts. But for some reason he has chosen to turn a blind eye to any evidence of pneumonic plague. He does not notice how often the victims are said to have succumbed in three days and if he meets with any reference to plague in cold weather he jumps to the conclusion that the disease must have been something else, preferably typhus. We are never told that the symptoms of typhus are unlike those of plague, except perhaps in some cases of septicaemic plague, which would be unlikely to occur in winter. It is true that in the later stages of typhus the tongue may bleed and cause spitting of blood but in typhus death very seldom ensues before the second week of illness. Shrewsbury's typhus theory, first advanced tentatively on page 104, soon becomes what might be called a creeping hypothesis; that is to say, it becomes more and more on later pages a statement of fact. But there is much evidence, all of it ignored by Shrewsbury, that the Great Pestilence of 1348—50 contained a high percentage of pneumonic cases and indeed that in many places the plague first appeared in its pneumonic form. This would easily account for the high mortality which Shrewsbury is anxious to whittle down. Some of the evidence comes from authors whom Shrewsbury himself quotes. The most explicit example is the account given, by the great medieval doctor Guy de Chauliac, of the outbreak at Avignon in 1348. It is worth quoting in full. 'The said mortality began with us in the month of January and lasted for the space of seven months. It was of two sorts: the first lasted two months [January and February], with continuous fever and expectoration of blood; and men died of it in three days.' This can refer only to pneumonic plague and in no way resembles typhus. 'The second lasted the remainder of the time, also with continuous fever and with external carbuncles and buboes, chiefly in the armpits or the groin, and men died of it in five days.' He even notes that the disease in its pulmonary form was thought more infectious.[6]

Numerous other chroniclers mention the coughing or spitting of blood, death after three days, or the winter incidence of the epidemic. They range from Constantinople, Sicily and Spain to Poland, Russia, Scotland and Ireland. The same phenomena are noted by the Byzantine Emperor John Cantacuzene and the Byzantine chronicler Nicephorus Gregoras.[7] The same story is told by Michele Piazza and Gabriele de Musis describing the plague at Messina[8] and by Matteo Villani on the epidemic at Florence,[9] while other witnesses attest pneumonic cases in Venice and in Piacenza.[10] For Avignon, de Chauliac's account is substantiated by an anonymous Flemish canon and by Raymond Chalin de Vinario, physician there to three Popes.[11] From Montpellier Simon de Covino (in Latin hexameters) and from Paris Jean de Venette take up the tale.[12] In Almeria the Spanish Moor Ibn Khatimah records the coughing up of blood, as does his colleague Ibn-al-Khatib.[13] We hear also of pneumonic symptoms from Germany, Norway, Russia and even from Poland which escaped relatively lightly.[14] For Great Britain, admittedly, there is no direct testimony describing lung cases, but we do hear of death in three days and, for many parts of the country, of plague during the winter.[15] But from Ireland we have Friar John Clyn of Kilkenny, himself a victim of the plague, who is quoted by Professor Shrewsbury. The friar tells us, though the professor fails to say so, that 'some died spitting blood'.[16]

What is the cause of Shrewsbury's myopia? Perhaps it came upon him at the moment when (on page 6) he delivered himself of the dictum 'pneumonic plague cannot occur in the absence of the bubonic form and it cannot persist as an independent form of plague'. This is untrue; and Professor Shrewsbury knew it when, in another book, he wrote of the great Manchurian outbreak of 1910–11 that the 'epidemic was exclusively one of pneumonic plague and was disseminated solely by human contacts'.[17] The Manchurian epidemic was indeed exclusively pneumonic, as was the slightly less destructive outbreak of 1920–1; and it could easily have spread far beyond Manchuria but for the heroic counter-measures taken by the great Chinese doctor Wu Lien Teh who was most fortunately put in charge. Wu Lien Teh's classic treatise on pneumonic plague[18] is significantly absent from Shrewsbury's very extensive bibliography.

Once he has decided to ignore pneumonic plague the professor gets well into his stride. It was, he argues, beyond the powers of a purely bubonic epidemic, which he claims it was, to kill nearly as many people in the Great Pestilence as historians have supposed. Henceforward no holds are barred if they can be used to minimize the death roll. For instance, on page 79 we are asked to disbelieve the fact that in the diocese of Lichfield at least 184 out of 459 livings became vacant by death during the pandemic and that new incumbents had to be instituted by Bishop Norburg (Lichfield provides more exact and reliable figures than any other diocese). The ground given for disbelief is a suggestion that if these deaths had been due to plague the bishop would have panicked and refused to institute. It has not occurred to the professor that a medieval bishop might have been courageous, conscientious or possibly foolhardy.[19]

Shrewsbury casts further doubt on the statistics for clerical mortality on the somewhat doubtful grounds that most clergymen would be elderly and that plague has allegedly a preference for killing those aged 10 to 35. He seems to forget that monasteries have novices and that many parishes have quite youthful curates. In any case, the expectation of life in the middle ages was so low that relatively few people in any walk of life could have been very elderly. Moreover, pneumonic plague is no respecter of persons and will kill anyone of any age who has inhaled infected droplets. And as to bubonic plague, we read in Stitt's *Tropical Diseases* that 'age, sex, race and occupation are not predisposing factors of importance in connection with plague', and that if in some outbreaks more cases do occur in middle life this is almost certainly due to greater exposure to infection.[20] It might also be mentioned that between 1949 and 1965 seven of the eighteen confirmed plague cases in New Mexico were among children under ten.[21]

The professor's eccentricities all arise from the knowledge he claims to have of 'the invariable aetiology' of bubonic plague and of its unvarying relationship with rodent enzootics. But the aetiology of plague is not in fact quite so uniform as Shrewsbury says. In 1937 Nasik in Western India had a human plague incidence' of 363 per thousand inhabitants but all the black rats examined were found to be immune; and Bombay once in this century produced no infected rats for two years, out of 2,000 examined daily, while the human plague rate was 199.8 per mille.[22]

Shrewsbury's final verdict on the Great Pestilence (he is technically if pedantically right in refusing to call it the Black Death since the term was not used before the sixteenth century) is that it killed perhaps a twentieth of the population of Britain. It may be that earlier estimates, ranging between a third and a half, are too high. But 5 per cent will hardly do. Even if the epidemic had been purely bubonic this figure is improbable since, as Shrewsbury shows in later chapters, the sixteenth and seventeenth century plagues, which were mainly bubonic, reduced the population of London by at least 20 per cent on each occasion. It is true that the population of fourteenth century England was mainly rural, widely scattered and not much given to travel—apart from pilgrimages, which, incidentally, have been great promoters of plague in modern India. But rats are not unknown in rural areas; and bubonic plague can travel in goods harbouring fleas, while pneumonic plague can go to any place whither an infected person carries it. Moreover, on Shrewsbury's own showing (p. 522) the highest death rate ever recorded anywhere was that for the remote and scattered Derbyshire village of Eyam in 1665 where five-sixths of the inhabitants died. It would seem then that the professor has done too much of a hatchet job on the traditional estimated for the Great Pestilence and that Ziegler's recent estimate of between 25 and 35 per cent is considerably more convincing.[23]

But Shrewsbury, having disposed of what he regards as the myth of the Black Death, has no inclination to rest on his laurels. He proceeds to pour cold water on the idea that plague kept on coming back to England during the century and a half after 1350, thereby keeping down the population growth. It may be significant that he does not appear to know Saltmarsh's justly famous article on 'Plague and Economic Decline in England in the later Middle Ages'[24] nor yet Bean's somewhat unconvincing reply to it.[25] Shrewsbury's main contention is that the country would have had to be constantly re-infected by fresh importations of plague-bearing rats. He has not thought of the possibility that England might well have become an enzootic area in which some rats at any given time are diseased. This is odd since he knows very well that in other parts of the world plague has taken permanent root and produced notorious enzootic or endemic centres. Indeed he argues, mistakenly as it happens, that India has always been one such centre from which Europe has drawn its periodic re-infections.

Besides, if England became, as obviously it did, a permanently enzootic area in the seventeenth century, why should it not have done so two centuries earlier? That plague was endemic, or at least enzootic in London, needing no imported re-infections, for more than half a century before 1665 is abundantly clear from the annual mortality bills. For the years 1603 to 1666 inclusive only sixteen years show less than ten plague deaths in London, and of those, only three years (1629, 1633, 1635) record 'nil' (though 1634 has only one). Nineteen of the years in question record over 1,000 plague deaths and eight more have over 100, including 996 in 1643.[26]

Shrewsbury tells us ad nauseam that the evidence for recurrences of plague in Britain during the late fourteenth and throughout the fifteenth century is slight and suspect. We are told in particular that the many epidemics-which did admittedly occur were in all likelihood outbreaks of some other disease. But this assumes that our ancestors could not distinguish one disease from another. There is, however, considerable evidence to the contrary; and, after all, plague, at least in its bubonic form, it not difficult to recognise nor very easy to confuse with something else.

The earliest of all European plague treatises, by the Catalan doctor Jacme d'Agramont of Lerida (1348), distinguishes carefully between plague on the one hand and smallpox, measles, anthrax and goitre on the other.[27] Incidentally, Jacme notes that plague can 'specially affect the phlegm', that some victims can die almost suddenly with no obvious symptoms (which might happen in septicaemic cases), that the disease flourishes particularly near the coast and is more prevalent in some streets or houses than in others, and that it may well have some connexion with dirt.[28] Again, we know, from a treatise ascribed to 'John of Burgundy' and probably written before 1400, and also from certain German chronicles of the same period, that plague could clearly be distinguished from exanthematic typhus.[29] It was certainly so distinguished by the great Italian doctor Fracastoro (the earliest expert on syphilis and 'onlie begetter' of its name) who wrote in the early sixteenth century.[30]

Shrewsbury has of course to admit that in the sixteenth century plague undoubtedly recurred in Britain but he insists as usual that it must have been re-imported each time and will not allow that it could have become enzootic. It should perhaps be mentioned that he depends greatly on reiteration, believing apparently that what I tell you thirty times is true. His denial of the enzootic possibility is the more odd since his rather strange explanation of why plague finally left England after 1665 depends on the recognition of a permanent or chronic centre.

The argument, first advanced by Sir William Simpson in 1905,[31] is that the replacement of overland routes to Europe from the East by ships sailing round the Cape broke the chain of re-infection from the plague's eastern endemic foci. An infected rat or a blocked flea can easily travel in someone's saddle-bags, by camel. But both would die before a ship got round the Cape—although of course one plague rat could start an epizootic among the others in the ship. But the argument is based on a false premise. It assumes that the main sources of infection were the Indian ports and that they remained infectious after 1665 though no longer able to purvey infection to the West. This is unfortunate, since it seems that there was no plague in India from 1684 (or possibly 1702) until 1812, with the exception of two small areas (Garwhal and Kumaon) far inland at the foot of the Himalayas.[32] Bombay almost certainly had had no plague for well over two centuries before it was hit by the appalling outbreak of 1896, which is known to have reached it from Hong Kong. Moreover, the transfer from land to sea routes for oriental trade began early in the seventeenth century, well before plague turned back from Western Europe.[33] We might posit an alternative explanation, namely, that the absence of plague from eighteenth-century India led to its absence from eighteenth-century Europe. But this will not fit the facts, since plague was by no means absent from Eastern Europe throughout the eighteenth century. Russia and the Turkish Empire indeed had plenty of it but, in spite of considerable Baltic and Levantine trade, they did not infect north-western countries.

Lady Mary Wortley Montagu in 1717 was startled to find the plague all round her at Adrianople. 'We passed', she wrote,

through two or three towns most violently infected. In the very next house where we lay . . . two persons died of it. Luckily for me I was so well deceived that I knew nothing of the matter; and I was made to believe that our second cook who fell ill here had only a great cold. However . . . I am now let into the secret that he has had the plague.

But, with the ill-founded optimism so characteristic of her time, she also says,

Those dreadful stories you have heard of the plague have very little foundation in fact . . . I am convinced there is little more in it than a fever . . . I am persuaded it would be as easy to root it out here as out of Italy and France; but it does so little mischief, they are not very solicitous about it.[34]

Why then did the plague recede? There is a conventional view at which Shrewsbury glances a little cursorily. It is that plague disappeared from England through her invasion by the brown or Norway rat, leading to the virtual disappearance of the black one. Shrewsbury does not tell us very clearly what he thinks of this hypothesis and he does not discuss the pros and cons. But they are worth examining.

It is true that, although both types of rat are susceptible to plague (the brown one indeed usually gets it first)[35] the brown rat is less dangerous to man since he lives further from human dwellings and his fleas have slightly less appetite for human blood. It is also true that, on his arrival in Britain, he drove away most of his far more dangerous black cousins. But most authorities agree that *Rattus norvegicus,* the brown rat, did not reach the British Isles in any force until about 1730, for which reason he is often called the Hanover rat.[36] But plague had left England by 1671. Moreover, though Shrewsbury does not mention this, it had left most of North-West Europe even earlier—Scotland, Ireland and probably Wales by 1651, Denmark by 1654, Sweden and South Italy by 1657, the Netherlands by 1666, France and Switzerland by 1669.[37] The disease in fact was rapidly withdrawing and by the eighteenth century had virtually retired into Russia and the Balkans— apart from its severe but localized raids on Marseilles in 1720 and Messina in 1743.

It looks therefore as though some other explanation is required. No doubt, the more hygienic habits that were very slowly coming in would have reduced the incidence of fleas. Buildings of brick and stone provide less harbourage for rats than lath and plaster and are less easy for a rat to gnaw. But the poor of North-West Europe were not much cleaner in 1700 than in 1600 and not much better housed. It is possible of course that the disease was still present among the rodents but had declined in virulence or infectivity. Some experts, however, have doubted whether the virulence of *Pasteurella pestis* does significantly vary.[38] But Shrewsbury ignores this and from time to time assumes that the virulence periodically declined—hence his belief in the necessity for the re-infection of an area from outside, unless the area is India.

What is perhaps more likely, though Shrewsbury never considers it, is that either the rodent or the human population of North-West Europe, including Britain, had by about 1670 begun to 'breed immune'. In other words, only stocks with acquired or inherited immunity were now surviving, the susceptible having died out. The immunity could have been one or both of two different kinds—immunity to plague or immunity to flea-bite. Although second attacks of the disease can and do occur they are not very common and survival from one infection almost certainly confers a considerable degree of resistance. And some people, doubtless, have a natural or inborne immunity. The rodents, certainly, have in some areas been known to 'breed immune'.[39] But, more important, there is reason to believe that some men are much less liable to flea-bite than other men and that this uninviting quality in their blood is often hereditary.[40]

One possible weakness in Shrewsbury's general argument is that he concentrates so entirely on rat-borne disease, and on the presumptive presence or movement of rats, that he is led into ignoring or distorting some important evidence, particularly on plague in the Dark Ages. He admits that rats must have been present in the Middle East to cause the great pandemic of Justinian's time so unmistakably described by Procopius; and he admits rather grudgingly that the rat may in that century have got as far as Southern France. But he insists that it cannot have reached the British Isles and he therefore denies that the pestilence referred to by Bede and by certain Irish annals was plague. This, as Shrewsbury knows, is controversial. His argument for the non-existence of rats in sixth-century Britain is an argument from silence. They do not occur· in British records until they appear in an illustration to the *Book of Kells*. But he forgets possibly how few British records before that there actually are. We are told, somewhat reluctantly (on page 12), of the fifth-century Irish bishop said much later by Giraldus Cambrensis to have had his library destroyed by 'majores mures' vulgarly called 'rati'.[41] Incidentally, one would like to know how early we can date the legends of the Pied Piper of Hamelin and of the tenth-century Bishop Hatto who was eaten by rats.

Here, it seems, Shrewsbury has exposed another of his blind spots. He ignores the fact that the ancients had no separate words for mice and rats. 'Mures' had to do duty for both. He argues therefore that rats were unknown in the classical world; and he follows Hinton in believing that they were only introduced to the West at the time of the Crusades.[42] But Hinton himself, in a footnote, draws attention to two bronze statuettes of rats (one of *R.rattus* and one of *R.norvegicus*) found in a first-century site at Rome.[43] Moreover, rat skeletons have been excavated in Pompeii and a rat is depicted on a Roman tomb at Rheims dating from the second century A.D. Besides, Strabo, writing in the first century B.C., says that in Spain 'mures' often cause pestilence and that the Romans in Cantabria (that is, Asturias) advertised for a 'muricidus' during one such outbreak. Cats would normally suffice as mouse-killers and, in any case, mice very rarely cause plague.[44] The great Arab physician Avicenna (980–1037 A.D.) also noted that in Spain plague and dead rats went together.[45]

Again, it is clear that the sixth-century pestilence described by Gregory of Tours was bubonic and therefore rat-borne, since Gregory calls it 'lues inguinaria', that is, 'groin plague'. Shrewsbury has to admit that the disease and therefore the rats did reach the South of France but Gregory records it as far north as Bourges, Chalon and Dijon.[46] He also says that in his time a brazen rat was found in a drain near Paris, 'after which innumerable rats were seen in the city'.[47] The word he used ('clerem' for 'glirem') usually means a dormouse, but a brazen dormouse seems slightly improbable, as does a plague of dormice in a city.

Since he will not allow rats north of the Riviera, Shrewsbury insists that the British epidemic described by Bede cannot have been plague. But this is to ignore the fact that in Bede's Life of St. Cuthbert we are told that the Saint once had a groin bubo and suffered from the same disease that 'carried off so many in his time'.[48] Nor will Shrewsbury allow that the Irish epidemic of 664 can have been plague, on the grounds that it was called 'the Yellow Plague', although MacArthur has shown that this phrase was a much later interpolation in the relevant chronicle.[49]

Scholarly caution or even scepticism may be justified in the cases of Gregory of Tours or Bede but to carry scepticism into twentieth-century medical history is perhaps to carry it too far. Shrewsbury (pp. 506–10) will have nothing to do with the generally accepted view that there was plague, and pneumonic plague at that, in Suffolk between 1906 and 1918. He grants that plague rats were found in the area at the time, the infection having possibly arrived in a grain ship from the Argentine. And he has already admitted (pp. 428 and 531) the recurrence of plague in Glasgow in 1900 (36 cases, with 16 deaths) and in Liverpool in 1901 (11 cases, with 8 deaths). But he rules out Suffolk on the grounds that the dangerous black rat had long since been ousted by the brown. But this can hardly have applied in Liverpool and Glasgow; and to say this is to ignore two important facts. The first is that the black rat flourishes better than the brown on shipboard and is therefore liable to be found in ports and coastal areas. The second fact is that since 1895 the black rat, together with his flea (*Xenopsylla cheopis*) is known to have been recovering lost ground. In 1937, 90 per cent of the rats examined in London were found to be black although in 1911 all the rats there had been brown.[50]

Let us look in detail at the Suffolk story. In the winter of 1906-7 there were eight cases of severe illness among poor cottagers at Shotley, Suffolk, five of them pneumonic and fatal. In the winter of 1909—10 at Trimley, two miles away, there were eight more cases with five deaths, some of them pneumonic and four (including the first patient) showing buboes. In September 1910 at Freston there were four more cases, in a family of seven, all pneumonic and all fatal, plus one nurse who died also. *Pasteurella pestis* was found post mortem in two of these patients and possibly in a third. In 1911 a seaman died admittedly of plague in Shotley barracks, and in 1918 there were two more alleged plague deaths less than two miles away. Thus we have in all 24 cases with 18 deaths.[51]

According to Shrewsbury no outbreak of plague has been diagnosed as such 'on flimsier evidence' (p. 508). He wants the bubonic cases to be bovine tuberculosis (which does not kill very quickly) and the rest typhus—partly on the grounds of one patient's having had red spots (a possible symptom of septicaemic plague), partly on the grounds of winter incidence but mainly on the peculiar grounds that if the patients had fleas they might equally have been lousy, and typhus is of course a louse-borne disease. The pneumonic symptoms are inevitably swept aside; and Shrewsbury has, as usual, forgotten that pneumonic plague flourishes best in cold weather. We might agree with him in regretting that more bacteriological examinations were not made. But he, on his side, might be asked to remember that typhus victims do not invariably die in three days coughing bloody sputum.

Scholarly caution is always necessary. We must not, for example, make too much of a remark in Webster's *The White Devil*, 'Equally mortal with a winter plague',[52] since 'plague' here may merely mean disease. And it is going too far to assert, as had been done in a standard medical textbook, that there were forty-one known epidemics of plague before the Christian era.[53] But there is no need to carry caution to the point of mania, which Professor Shrewsbury would appear to have done. The sometimes acrid or cantankerous tone of voice he uses, the amount of sheer assertion and reiteration in his argument, the over-emphasis of his points, the implication that he alone knows the aetiology of plague, the ill-disguised contempt for most earlier authorities are all suggestive of a certain obsessiveness. The obsession or mania might be called 'pesticidal'. All through his book he is out to minimize and if possible to scotch any alleged case of plague that he can and, whenever possible, to turn it into something else, preferably typhus. And this, as we have seen, will not always do.

All this may seem ungracious and ungrateful, perhaps merely niggling or even captious, in the case of a book embodying so much arduous and detailed work, much of it undoubtedly scholarly and much of it valuable in many ways. But the reviewer's first duty is to truth, and unfortunately many of the views advanced with such confidence by Professor Shrewsbury are, to say the least, not proven; and heresies setting themselves up as new and definitive orthodoxies invite a little persecution.

Notes

1.   W.G. Bell, *The Great Plague of London* (London, 1924), p. 325.
2.   Cf. C.F. Mullett, *The Bubonic Plague and England* (Lexington, Kentucky, 1956), pp. 4 and 196, and Bell, op. cit., passim.
3.   Bell, op. cit. pp. 148–9 and 242.
4.   Wu Lien Teh, J.W.H. Chun, R. Pollitzer and C.Y. Wu, *Plague. A Manual for Medical and Public Health Workers* (Shanghai, 1936), p. 269. Cf. L.F. Hirst, *The Conquest of Plague. A Study in Epidemiology* (Oxford, 1953), pp. 322–4, 328, 331.
5.   Cf. Hirst, op. cit. pp. 33–5 and 222.
6.   Guy de Chauliac, *La Grande Chirurgie* (1363), E. Nicaise (ed.) (Paris, 1890), pp. 169–70 (my translation). See also Hirst, op. cit. p. 32; A. Castiglioni, *A History of Medicine,* E. B. Krumbhaar (tr. and ed.) (New York, 1958), pp. 357–8; R. Crawfurd, *Plague and Pestilence in Literature and Art* (Oxford, 1914), pp. 120–1.
7.   See C.S. Bartsocas, 'Two Fourteenth Century Greek Descriptions of the Black Death', in *Journal of the History of Medicine and Allied Sciences,* xxi (1966), 394–400. Cf. Crawfurd, op. cit. p. 112; A. Jessop, 'The Black Death in East Anglia', in *The Coming of the Friars* (London, 1930), p. 173; Sir William Simpson, *A Treatise of Plague* (Cambridge, 1905), pp. 21–2; and G. Deaux, *The Black Death* (London, 1969), pp. 47–8.
8.   Cited in Castiglioni, op. cit. p. 355; R. Hare, *Pomp and Pestilence* (London, 1954), p. 91; and F.A. Gasquet, *The Black Death* (London, 1908), pp. 14–15 and 18–19.
9.   Cited in Jessop, op. cit. p. 172.
10. Cited in Wu Lien Teh, *A Treatise on Pneumonic Plague* (League of Nations Health Organization, Geneva, 1926), p. 4.
11. Cited in Deaux, op. cit. pp. 100–2; Crawfurd, op. cit. pp. 121–2; and P. Ziegler, *The Black Death* (London, 1969), p. 22. Cf. J.F.K. Hecker, *Epidemics of the Middle Ages,* tr. B. G. Babington (London, 1859), pp. 9–10; and Sir George Newman, *The Rise of Preventive Medicine* (Oxford, 1932), p. 119.
12. See Deaux, op. cit. pp. 95–6 and 105; Ziegler, op. cit. pp. 19–20; *The Chronicle of Jean de Venette* (tr. J. Birdsall), R.A. Newhall (ed.) (Columbia University, 1953), pp. 48–50.
13. See Ziegler, op. cit. p. 115; B.L. Gordon, *Mediaeval and Renaissance Medicine* (New York, 1959), p. 457; A.M. Campbell, *The Black Death and Men of Learning* (Columbia University, 1931), pp. 62, 78–80, 83–4, 87.
14. Hecker, op. cit. pp. 6–8. Cf. Wu Lien Teh, op. cit. p. 5.
15. See Henry Knighton, *Chronicon,* J. R. Lumby (ed.) Rolls Series (London, 1895), II, 61; Robert of Avesbury, *De Gestis Mirabilibus Regis Edwardi Tertii,* E.M. Thompson (ed.), Rolls Series (London, 1889), pp. 405–7; Geoffrey le Baker, *Chronicon,* E.M. Thompson (ed.) (Oxford, 1889), pp. 98–9. Cf. Ziegler, op. cit. pp. 19, 157, 161–2, 184, 190, 198–9 and Deaux, op. cit. pp. 123 and 130–1.
16. *The Annals of Ireland by Friar John Clyn,* R. Butler (ed.) (Dublin, 1849), p. vi. Cf. Hirst, op. cit. pp. 13–14.
17. J.F.D. Shrewsbury, *The Plague of the Philistines* (London, 1964), p. 21.
18. Wu Lien Teh, *A Treatise on Pneumonic Plague* (League of Nations Health Organization, Geneva, 1926).
19. Cf. p. 71 for a similar observation on Bishop Trilleck of Hereford.
20. Op. cit. Revised R.P. Strong (7th ed., London, 1945), p. 677. Cf. H.C. Trowell and D.B. Jelliffe, *Diseases of Children in the Subtropics and Tropics* (London, 1958), p. 604.

21. R.W. Collins et al. in *U.S. Public Health Reports,* LXXXII (1967), 1077—99.
22. See Sir H.H. Scott, *A History of Tropical Medicine,* II (London, 1942), 767; Wu Lien Teh et al., op. cit. pp. 300 and 418, and Stitt, op. cit. p. 671.
23. Ziegler, op. cit. pp. 228—30.
24. J. Saltmarsh in *The Cambridge Historical Journal,* VII (1941), 23—41.
25. J.M.W. Bean, 'Plague, Population and Economic Decline in the later Middle Ages', in *The Economic History Review,* 2nd ser., xv (1963), 423 ff.
26. Simpson, op. cit. pp. 29—30. Cf. C. Creighton, *A History of Epidemics in Britain,* I (Cambridge, 1891), 533.
27. *Regiment de Preservacio a Epidemia o Pestilencia e Mortaldats,* tr. M.L. Duran-Reynals and C.E.A. Winslow, in *Bulletin of the History of Medicine,* XXIII, I (1949), 57 — 89.
28. ıbid. pp. 61, 62, 68—70, 73, 75.
29. See · A. Hirsch, *Handbook of Geographical and Historical Pathology,* tr. C. Creighton. (New Sydenham Society, London, 1883) I, 499, 546—9. Cf. Creighton, op. cit. I, pp. 208—14, and Mullett, op. cit. pp. 32—3.
30. See *Works* (Venice, 1584), p. 87. Cf. Hirsch, op. cit. p. 499.
31. Op. cit. pp. 32—3 and 37.
32. See Wu Lien Teh et al., op. cit. p. 5; .M. Greenwood, *Epidemics and Crowd Diseases* (London, 1935), pp. 295—6; Simpson, op. cit. pp. 44—5.
33. See Wu Lien Teh et al., op. cit. p. 8.
34. To Miss Sarah Chiswell, 1 Apr. 1717. *Letters,* R. Brimley Johnson (ed.) London, Everyman, 1906), p. 123.
35. Hirst, op. cit. pp. 137—41.
36. Ibid, pp. 123—4. Cf. Wu Lien Teh et al., op. cit. p. 9.
37. Scott, op. cit. II, 708—9; Simpson, op. cit. p. 33; Hirst, op. cit. p. 86.
38. See Wu Lien Teh et al, op. cit. pp. 92—6, and W.W.C. Topley and G.S. Wilson, *The Principles of Bacteriology and Immunology,* II (London, 1929), 1070. But cf. Hirst, op. cit. pp. 258—60 and 266—7.
39. Wu Lien Teh et al., op. cit. pp. 227—8 and 398.
40. I owe this information to an unpublished lecture which I heard given by the late Dr. G.S. Graham-Smith, formerly of the Indian Plague Commission.
41. Cited in Hirst, op. cit. p. 123.
42. M.A.C. Hinton, *Rats and Mice as Enemies of Mankind* (London, 1918), p. 4. Cf. G.A.H. Barratt-Hamilton and M.A.C. Hinton, *A History of British Mammals* (London, 1916). pt. 18.
43. Cited in Hirst, op. cit. p. 124.
44. Ibid. pp. 124—5. See Strabo·III, iv, 18.
45. Gordon, op. cit. p. 458. Cf. A.M. Campbell, op. cit. p. 35.
46. *History of the Franks,* tr. O.M. Dalton, II (Oxford, 1927), 141 (Book IV, xxiv, 31).
47. Ibid p. 358 (Book VIII, xxx, iii).
48. Cited in Sir William MacArthur, 'Historical Notes on Some Epidemic Diseases connected with Jaundice', *British Medical Journal,* xiii, 2 (1957), 148—9.
49. Ibid.
50. Hirst, op. cit. pp. 345—7.
51. See H. T. Bulstrode, *40th Annual Report of the Medical Officer, Local Government Board* (London, 1910), Appendix, A.3; A. Eastwood and F. Griffith in *Journal of Hygiene,* xiv (Cambridge, 1914), 285. Cf. Greenwood, op. cit. pp. 292—3; Hirst, op. cit. pp. 337—8, Scott, op. cit. II, 711—2; Wu Lien Teh, *Pneumonic Plague,* pp. 50—51 and Saltmarsh, op. cit. p. 32.
52. Op. cit. V, viii. Cf F.P. Wilson, *The Plague in Shakespeare's London* (Oxford 1963).
53. Topley and Wilson, op. cit. II, 1057.

Manner of burying the dead at Holy Well Mount, near London, during the plague of 1665

The Local Incidence of Epidemic Disease:

the Case of Bristol 1540-1650

Paul Slack

As recent articles in *Local Population Studies* have suggested, the study of 'crisis mortality' is one of the more rewarding tasks for the student of population and one of the most valuable for the historian of pre-industrial societies. It is also an area in which the local historian has a vital role to play in collecting and interpreting the evidence. As Dr. Schofield has shown,[1] simple calculations of crisis mortality based on aggregative analysis of burial registers enable us to measure the relative severity of epidemic disease from parish to parish; and the local differences which emerge both illustrate the conditions in which disease flourished and point to broader social and economic variations from locality to locality. In the case of a large town with several surviving parish registers, we can even study these differences in mortality within a single local community and use them as one indicator of the varying quality of life in an early modern town. From this point of view the large number of parishes in several English towns, which in other circumstances hinders the work of the urban historian, becomes a definite advantage. The purpose of this article is to show the sort of conclusions and problems which may arise from work of this kind by means of one small case-study.

Sixteenth-century Bristol was both a major port and an industrial centre. With a population of about 11,000 it was one of the largest provincial towns, containing 18 parishes, 12 of whose registers survive.[2] (See Map Fig. 1.) Inevitably a town of this kind suffered frequent outbreaks of plague and its civic annalists did not fail to record the fact. Epidemics were especially frequent at the beginning of the period. There was a 'plague of pestilence' in 1535, a 'great plague' in 1544-5 and 'the greatest mortality by pestilence in Bristol that any man knew' in 1551-2.[3] Parish registers can tell us nothing about the first, however, and only three registers for parishes in the centre of the town have entries for the others. But comparison of burials in the epidemic years with the annual average for a more normal period[4] suggests serious mortality (Table I).

Fig. 1 : Bristol

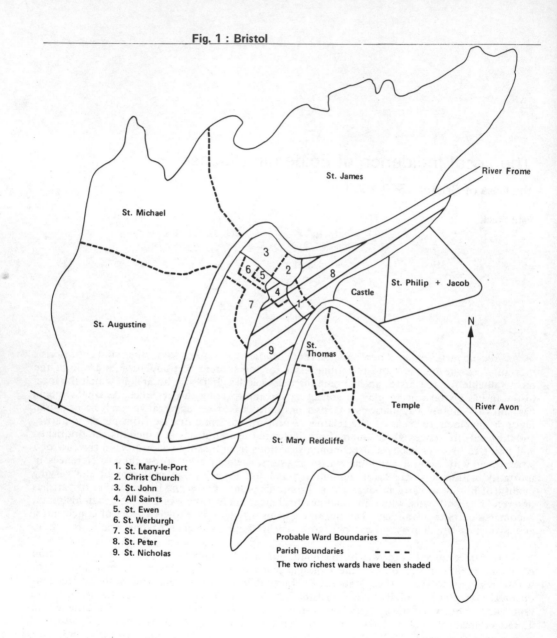

River Frome

St. James

St. Michael

3

6 5 2

8

St. Philip + Jacob

Castle

4

1

7

St. Augustine

N

9

St.
Thomas

Temple

River Avon

St. Mary Redcliffe

1. St. Mary-le-Port
2. Christ Church
3. St. John
4. All Saints
5. St. Ewen
6. St. Werburgh
7. St. Leonard
8. St. Peter
9. St. Nicholas

Probable Ward Boundaries ————
Parish Boundaries – – – –
The two richest wards have been shaded

Table I

Parish	Annual Average Burials 1539-43 + 1546-50 a	Aug. 1544 - July 1545		1552	
		Burials b	Ratio b/a	Burials c	Ratio c/a
St. Ewen	2.6	20	7.7	-	-
St. Nicholas	28.9	-	-	168	5.8
Christ Church	12.0	71	5.9	71	5.9

Between August 1544 and July 1545 burials in the parish of St. Ewen reached almost eight times the average, while in Christ Church and St. Nicholas's in the calendar year 1552 the number of burials was nearly six times the annual average. In St. Ewen's there were twenty burials in 1544-5, in a parish which in 1547 had only fifty-six communicants.[5] In each case the monthly distribution of burials, reaching a peak in the late autumn, would indicate an outbreak of bubonic plague, although the second epidemic was also preceded by a rise in burials in St. Nicholas's in July 1551, perhaps as a consequence of the 'sweating sickness'. The evidence is fragmentary, but two successive epidemics must have brought a crisis of major proportions to the central parishes of Bristol in these years.

There were three later better-documented outbreaks of bubonic plague before the civil war: in 1565, 1575 and 1603-4. Near-contemporary sources now provided figures for the total number of casualties. The plague of 1565 was said to have caused 2,070 deaths and that of 1575 2,000. For the 1603-4 epidemic, the chronicler claimed some statistical validity: the number dying between 18 July 1603 and February 1605 'according to the Church books and printed tickets' was '2,956, whereof of the plague 2,600'.[6]

Although these printed bills of mortality do not survive, it is possible to check the above figures with the registers of nine of the eighteen parishes of Bristol (shown in Table III below.) The chantry certificates suggest that these parishes contained rather less than two thirds of the communicants in the town. Since they included a large part of the suburbs, whose population may have been growing towards the end of the sixteenth century, this proportion is likely to have increased by 1603. But it can be used to provide a crude multiplier to convert the aggregate burials in the nine parishes into totals for Bristol as a whole. The totals arrived at are 1,800 for each of the calendar years 1565 and 1575, and 2,200 for the year from August 1603 to July 1604 when the plague had a noticeable effect on burials. Unlike similar assertions elsewhere, the figures presented in the Bristol annals do not seem to be grossly exaggerated. The total population of the town in 1547 has been put at roughly 11,000 and by 1603 it may have risen to 12,000.[7] In each of the three epidemics, therefore, the mortality rate may have been between sixteen and eighteen per cent.

There were no further major outbreaks of plague for nearly four decades after 1604. It is surprising that the epidemics in London in 1625 and 1636 were not duplicated later in Bristol as those of 1563 and 1603 had been, and the reasons for this are obscure. But it was not the result of good management. Although watchmen were appointed at the gates and ships inspected on the quay,[8] the disease in fact entered the town. Houses had to be quarantined in St. Thomas's parish and Temple in 1626 and burials rose in other parts of the town in the plague months of the next three years.[9] Between 1637 and 1639 the disease was more serious, requiring a pesthouse for the infected and payments to the sick in Temple and St. Mary Redcliffe.[10] But the annual number of burials did not reach twice the average in any parish. In both the 1620s and 1630s there were apparently sporadic cases of plague over several years, as if the disease were temporarily endemic in the town, but no major epidemic developed.

Whatever the causes of this interlude may have been, it was brought to an abrupt end by the civil war and two sieges in succession. At the end of 1641 there was already 'sickness' among soldiers in the castle and by the summer of 1642 it had spread into several parishes around.[11] In 1643 when royalist armies besieged Bristol mortality increased still further, probably as a result of typhus. A parliamentary tract significantly complained that the soldiers who took the town in July infested their beds 'with lice. So that the houses where they quartered are like Goales (sic) for nastinesse'.[12] Two years later, during the second siege, there was an even more serious epidemic when bubonic plague returned.[13] In the two years 1643 and 1645 nearly 2,800 people were buried in ten parishes where the normal annual average was 310. We have no means of knowing what the population of these parishes was, but it cannot have been more than about 10,000. These epidemics together caused a more serious loss of population than any in the period, with the possible exception of the plagues of 1544 and 1552.

Outbreaks of bubonic plague in Bristol were thus irregular in their occurrence and extremely variable in their effect on mortality. Even more interesting and certainly less speculative than attempts to calculate gross mortality figures, however, are the variations which emerge between parishes and their apparent coincidence in many cases with social class differences. For plague mortality was not spread evenly over the town. In 1603-4, for example, burials rose to ten times the annual average in St. James's parish, yet to only 2.4 times the average in Christ Church. In order to appreciate the significance of such differences we must first try to rank the parishes in order of wealth. There are several possible ways of doing this, depending on available source materials. Local poor rate assessments may be used to compare the number of those receiving relief with the number of those contributing towards it, and the ratios from different parishes can be compared. Subsidy assessments for different parishes, especially those of the 1520s, might be used with the acreages of parishes or the number of communicants in the chantry certificates to provide a rough index of wealth per acre or per person in each parish. None of these methods is infallible; neither can they precisely reflect the social make-up of a parish in which there might be extremes of wealth and poverty. But when taken together and when applied to several towns in this period, they agree in suggesting a concentration of the wealthier classes in the central parishes of an urban community and the congregation of the poor on its outskirts or in its suburbs.

The evidence for Bristol, though in this respect less good than for some other urban centres, in no way conflicts with this broad generalisation. Unfortunately the subsidy assessments subdivide the town into wards and not parishes, but the 1524 assessment names the parish churches in each ward and it seems probable that most of the area of each parish fell in the same ward as its parish church. The calculations in Table II, comparing the 1524 and 1591 subsidy assessments[14] with the chantry returns, may then be used to show variations in

Table II   Wealth of Bristol Wards

Wards	Subsidy assessment[1] (a) (b) 1524 1591	Parish Churches in 1524	1547 'houseling' people (c) ward total	Wealth 1524 1591 a/c b/c
St. Mary-le-Port	1865 293	St. Mary St. Peter	580	3.2 0.51
All Saints	2867 588	All Saints St. Nicholas	980	2.9 0.6
St. Ewen	1961 258	St. Ewen St. Werburgh St. Leonard St. Stephen St. Lawrence	897	2.2 0.29
Holy Trinity	1733 404	Christ Church St. John St. Augustine St. Michael St. James St. Philip	1839[2]	0.94 0.22
Redcliffe	932 274	St. Mary St. Thomas Temple	1680	0.56 0.16

1 To the nearest shilling.
2 There is no chantry return for St. Augustine's parish: this ward was therefore rather more populous and less wealthy than these figures suggest.

wealth between the rich central wards of St. Mary-le-Port and All Saints, and the poor suburb of Redcliffe across the Avon. These figures, however, must mask variations within wards and particularly in the large ward of Holy Trinity. Here it seems probable from the topography of the town and from later evidence that the central parish of Christ Church was closer to the neighbouring parishes of All Saints and St. Mary than to the suburban parishes of St. James and St. Philip in its social composition.[15]

Accepting these conclusions, the parishes may then be ranked roughly in order of wealth and the relative severity of the three outbreaks of plague after 1560 compared by means of ratios of epidemic to normal burials (Table III). It is immediately clear that variations in mortality do not exactly follow variations in wealth. Neither would we expect them to do so, since social class was not the sole variable involved. The disease was carried relatively slowly

Table III Bristol: Burials in the Plagues of 1565, 1575, and 1603-4 (Aug-July).

Parishes in approx. descending order of wealth.	1565			1575		1603-4		
	Burials	Normal Annual Average [1]	Ratio	Burials	Ratio	Burials	Normal Annual Average [2]	Ratio
	a	b	a/b	c	c/b	d	e	d/e
All Saints	32	3.8	8.4	16	4.2	18	4.8	3.8
St. Nicholas	122	23.4	5.2	157	6.7	124	25.4	4.9
St. Ewen	-	2.6	-	10	3.8	-	-	-
St. Werburgh	32	5.2	6.2	15	2.9	35	6.6	5.5
St. Stephen	164	22.9	7.2	197	8.6	188	33.4	5.6
Christ Church	93	12.6	7.4	99	7.9	45	17.6	2.4
St. John	93	10.7	8.5	60	5.6	113	11.1	10.2
St. Augustine	-	-	-	-	-	93	12.8	7.3
St. Philip & Jacob	-	-	-	-	-	302	35.2	8.6
St. Mary Redcliffe	209	24.1	8.7	217	9.0	277	34.6	8.0
St. James	170	20.8	8.2	160	7.7	310 [3]	30.3	10.2
Temple	201	20.4	9.9	221	10.8	263	30.8	8.5

1. For the years 1566-74, except for St. Ewen's where gaps in the register dictate the choice of the years 1576-83.
2. For the years 1593-1602.
3. These burials are given in St. James's register for 1664-5, but there is some confusion in the dating.

through the town by rats and its effects tended to be most serious in parishes infected before October when climatic conditions were most favourable for the development of an epidemic.[16] Nevertheless there is some significant correlation at the extremes. Taking the three epidemics together, bubonic plague was most violent in the parishes of St. Mary Redcliffe, Temple and St. James. The two former, together with St. Thomas's, comprised the poorest ward in the town, on the southern bank of the Avon where industrial suburbs had grown up in the later Middle Ages.[17] On the other hand the central parishes of All Saints, St. Nicholas and St. Werburgh were normally those least severely affected. The heavy mortality in All Saints parish in 1565 provides the only major exception. Apart from this, the incidence of plague would appear to be to some degree related to the distribution of wealth.

The vital determinants behind this association were of course variations in standards of housing and hygiene which might attract or repel the rats and fleas which carried plague. The central parishes of the town were certainly its most fashionable areas. By the end of the sixteenth century St. Werburgh's even included a street of stone houses, which may have been relatively rat-proof. In St. Mary Redcliffe the extremes of wealth and poverty met side by side. There were some famous large merchants' houses, but this populous parish must also have contained many poor tenements.[18] The contrast between standards of hygiene in different parts of the town may have been even greater than variations in quality of housing, and also more important in determining the amount of contact between rats and men.[19] Visitors might praise the cleanliness of Bristol, with its paved streets and underground drains, a town 'where nothing is wanting....either for neatness or health'.[20]But such comments can have applied only to the central parishes. It is abundantly clear from presentments at the court leet that by the early seventeenth century the streets of Redcliffe ward were littered with decaying animal and vegetable matter. Conditions were so bad near St. Thomas's that 'people will hardly come to church by reason of the stench'.[21] In such an environment plague flourished.

If plague victims were unequally distributed between parishes, there were similar differences between streets within them. The 'Easter Books' of Christ Church parish, which survive for a few years at the end of the sixteenth century, allow us to reconstruct the incidence of mortality there. These record the names of all communicants contributing to the Easter collection, and they list the names street by street and apparently household by household. It is thus possible to discover the approximate location of the houses from which most of those buried in the plagues of 1575 and 1603 came.[22] (Table IV and Fig.2a and b). Wine Street and Broad Street were two of the main highways of the town, meeting at its centre, and they contained several large households, complete with servants and apprentices. But the 'Pithay' was a poor overcrowded alley leading to a workhouse in one of the towers in the walls. Although plague burials were scattered over a wide area and the disease moved haphazardly, sometimes missing out two or three households in its progress along a street, the Pithay lost a higher proportion of its inhabitants in both epidemics than any other part of the parish. This was especially so in the milder outbreak of 1603, but even in 1575 over half the burials in the first two months of the epidemic occurred here, and there were several others in the neighbouring houses of Wine Street. Bubonic plague was concentrated in the back street of this otherwise prosperous parish.

Table IV Christ Church Parish, Bristol: Communicants and Burials

Streets	Communicants listed at Easter					Burials[1]	
	1575	1576	1579	1601	1604	1575	1603
Broad St.	81	63	78	100	78	13	2
Wine St.	211	179	207	208	134	30	8
Tower Lane	46	36	32	27	27	4	1
The Pithay	71	60	68	79	67	26	24
Total	409	338	385	414	306	73	35
				Unidentified burials:		19	7

1. Burials for the months June-Dec. have been taken in each case.

Fig. 2: Christ Church Parish, Bristol a) Sketch Map

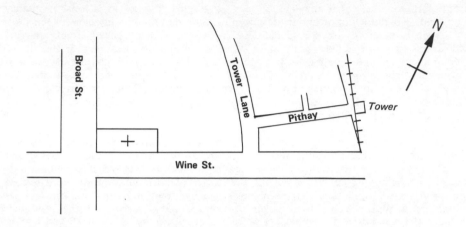

b) **Number of Burials in separate households 1575 and 1603 (June-December)**

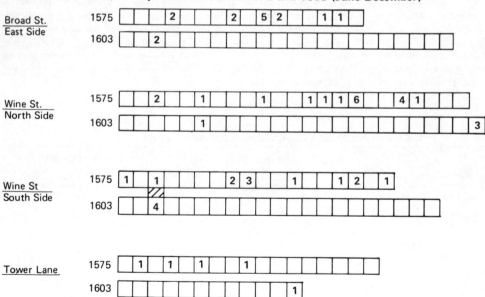

continued

continued

Pithay ? South Side

1575 2 1 1   1 1 3   3 2   1 3 1 1

1603   1   3 1   1 3   5 4   1

Pithay ? North Side

1575 1   3 2

1603   2   3

Each square represents one household unit. Where the same household was afflicted in both 1575 and 1603 the squares have been joined.

The Easter Books also provide some evidence for the effect of plague on fluctuations of population in this parish. The Books of 1575 and 1576 suggest a radical fall in the number of communicants within one year. But not all of this decline was due to epidemic mortality and there were significant differences from street to street. The fall in the numbers for Wine Street and Broad Street was largely a consequence of the flight of the most prosperous householders, for several names occur in both the listings of 1575 and 1579 which are not present in that of 1576. In the Pithay, on the other hand, most of the absentees were in fact victims of the plague and by Easter 1576 a few poor families had already migrated into the street to fill the vacant tenements. Others followed them in the years before 1579. The Easter Book of 1604, when compared with the burial register and the Book of 1601, suggests that the next plague had an even more disparate effect on different streets. Nearly one third of the adults in the two main streets appear to have fled, while there were already several newcomers in the alley behind them. The total population of the parish changed little over the period, but the turnover was much greater in the Pithay than elsewhere. This small parish may well illustrate in microcosm the effect of plague in the rich and poor areas of the town as a whole.

Plague thus had a socially selective impact on Bristol in these years, and this is important for any understanding of its demographic and economic effects. But it must not be over-stressed. No parish of the town entirely escaped the three epidemics between 1565 and 1604 and, as the Easter Books of Christ Church suggest, its movement from household to household might appear entirely random. Plague was a threat to a whole community, though not in reality of the same dimensions for all sections of it. Other epidemics provide instructive contrasts. A mortality crisis in 1597, which followed a series of bad harvests and was perhaps the consequence of diseases aggravated by malnutrition, affected only the poorer parishes of the town. Although the corporation arranged for the import of corn to combat the effects of scarcity,[23] the number of burials reached three times the average in the four parishes of St. John, St. Mary Redcliffe, Temple and St. Philip. Yet the wealthier parishes appear not to have been affected at all.[24]

Conversely, some periods of crisis mortality might affect the whole town indiscriminately. In 1643 the billeting of troops on Bristol in siege conditions spread disease, probably typhus, equally through all the parishes. Only Temple had significantly more burials than the others in 1643. Two years later, however, during the seond siege which was accom -

panied by an epidemic of bubonic plague, there was a clear distinction between rich and poor parishes (Table V). In a town full of soldiers and in conditions of siege, even typhus, a disease normally associated with poverty, might be dispersed over the whole city.[25] But the

Table V   Bristol: Burials in 1643 and 1645

Parishes in approx. descending order of wealth	Annual average no. of burials 1632-41 a	Burials 1643 b	Ratio b/a	Burials 1645 c	Ratio c/a
All Saints	8.2	24	2.9	14	1.7
St. Nicholas	39.0	114	2.9	88	2.3
St. Ewen	3.3	8	2.4	18	5.5
St. Werburgh	10.8	35	3.2	11	1.0
St. Stephen	47.1	134	2.8	226	4.8
Christ Church	24.1	69	2.9	-	-
St. John	21.3	75	3.5	89	4.2
St. Augustine	23.7	58	2.4	129	5.4
St. Philip and Jacob	56.3	77	1.4	-	-
St. Mary Redcliffe	59.4	184	3.1	466	7.8
St. James	51.5	169	3.1	416	8.1
Temple [1]	45.9	(240)	5.2	(372)	8.1

1. The register of Temple is badly mutilated, and figures taken from it are only approximate.

characteristic social incidence of bubonic plague remained. The epidemic of 1645 testifies even more clearly than its predecessors to the dependence of plague on rats and to its severity in areas where rats and men were in closest contact.

The history of plague in Bristol thus confirms the observations of contemporaries and the deductions which might be drawn from the disease's aetiology about its social incidence. It also raises associated problems which may be illuminated by similar work on other localities. For example, this evidence supports some of Professor Chambers' suggestions on the importance of the 'autonomous death-rate' in pre-industrial England.[26] Sporadic visitations of plague of unpredictable virulence were more frequent and more significant causes of crisis mortality in Bristol than fluctuations in food supplies. The dearth of the 1590s affected burials in only a minority of parishes and only the plague of 1552 seems to have been preceded by food-shortage in the town.[27] But as we have seen plague was not entirely 'autonomous' in its social incidence in urban communities. Hence it aggravated existing imbalances in health and mortality between rich and poor areas rather than creating new ones. Aggregative analysis shows that the ratio of baptisms to burials was greater in the central parishes of the town than in the suburbs even in normal years.[28] But the addition of crisis mortalities left poor parishes like St. Mary Redcliffe with a large surplus of burials over baptism over the whole period 1540-1650, while richer parishes like

St. Nicholas's still managed to produce a surplus of baptisms over burials. That the population of the poorer parishes did not decline before 1604 and even rose after that date, judging by the upward trend of baptisms and marriages, must be attributed to continuous and heavy immigration from rural areas. Plague thus exacerbated the particular character of urban suburbs with their constantly changing population, bringing with it all those social problems of poverty, crime and disease with which urban governors were increasingly concerned in this period.[29]

The Bristol evidence also raises questions concerning changes in the severity and incidence of plague over time. It is unfortunate that no registers survive for suburban parishes in the plague epidemics of the 1540s and 1550s, but the central parishes may have suffered relatively more severely then than in later outbreaks of the disease. For the disparity between rich and poor parishes appears to have increased in the later epidemics of the period, the contrast being much clearer in 1603-4 and 1645 than in 1565 (Tables III and V). There might be two possible reasons for a change in incidence of this kind. It is possible first that the social geography of the town was changing, that the social classes were becoming more concentrated in different areas, and that the central parishes were being rebuilt while the suburbs were turning into slums. There were contemporary comments that this was happening elsewhere in this period,[30] but detailed work on the social geography of Bristol would be needed to substantiate the suggestion.

The alternative explanation, a decline in the virulence of the disease, could also have played some part. The experience of Christ Church parish in the epidemics of 1575 and 1603-4 certainly suggests that the milder the epidemic, the more it was concentrated in poorer areas, and the plague of 1645, in which contrasts between parishes were greater than before, may have been less severe than in previous outbreaks. In eight parishes the ratios of burials in the epidemic years 1565, 1575, 1603-4 and 1645, to the normal annual average were respectively 7.8, 7.9, 7.5, and 5.9. But the latter figure is calculated from average burials for the 1630s when the population of these parishes may well have been higher than on the eve of the 1645 epidemic, after a prolonged siege and an outbreak of typhus. The Bristol evidence is inconclusive on this point.

Comparable work on the towns of Exeter and Norwich, however, has suggested a similar development in the incidence of plague from the mid-sixteenth century onwards, the concentration of mortality in suburban parishes being more conspicuous in epidemics after 1600 than before. It has also indicated a somewhat similar distribution of plague epidemics over time, although the actual dates of outbreaks do not exactly coincide.[31] The epidemics of the 1540s and 1550s seem to have been severe in each town. They were followed in Elizabeth's reign by two major epidemics in Exeter and three in Norwich. In the early seventeenth century there were outbreaks of declining virulence after the great plague of 1603-4, although neither town escaped as lightly as Bristol. Finally Exeter like Bristol suffered in 1643 from an epidemic, possibly of typhus, which was associated with civil war campaigns and which affected all parishes equally. Studies of other large towns would clearly be valuable as a means of testing some of the similarities to be observed here.

Equally, work along the same lines comparing burials in groups of rural parishes might suggest useful conclusions about the influence of size of settlement and transport facilities on the relative vulnerability of local communities to plague. Here, as in urban centres, plague can both be set in its social and topographical context and itself provide an index of the quality of life in different sorts of pre-industrial society. But whatever regularities and patterns may be observed by the historian, the irregular and haphazard features of the history of plague evident among the households of Christ Church parish and in the timing of major outbreaks in Bristol must also be remembered when considering its impact. For contemporaries the only obvious rules governing plague, apart from its tendency to concentrate among the poor, were cosmic and supernatural ones. The plague of 1565 might have been foreseen because it was preceded by 'red beams in length like the pole, and also fire like a Furnace' in the heavens; while in 1626 the inhabitants of Bristol felt themselves threatened by the divine scourges of 'Pestilence, famine and the sword' all at once, and the minister of St. Philip's based homilies on the town's 'miraculous' deliverance from the former for years afterwards.[32] The local incidence of bubonic plague was of more than demographic significance for the social history of sixteenth-and seventeenth-century towns.

Notes

1. *Local Population Studies,* 9, Autumn 1972. pp. 10-21.
2. The registers of St. James, St. Mary Redcliffe and St. Werburgh are still in the parish churches; that of Temple is also in St. Mary Redcliffe; the registers of All Saints, St. Nicholas, St. Philip and Jacob, St. Stephen, Christ Church, St. Ewen and St. John Baptist are in the Bristol Archives Office (hereafter B.A.O.). The register of St. Augustine's has been printed by the Bristol and Gloucestershire Archaeological Society (Records Section, iii,1956).
3. R. Ricart, *The Maire of Bristowe is Kalendar,* ed. L. Toulmin Smith (Camden Soc., New Series, v, 1872), p.53; 'Two Bristol Calendars', ed. A.E. Hudd, *Trans. of the Bristol and Glouc. Arch. Soc.,* xix (1894), 140-1; *Adams' Chronicle of Bristol,* ed. F.F. Fox, 1910, p.100.
4. As Dr. Schofield has pointed out (*LPS 9,* p. 11), the selection of years from which to calculate the 'normal' annual average presents problems. Since the later part of this article tries to measure differences in the severity of epidemics between parishes, the inclusion of an epidemic year in any moving average seems inadvisable, for it would reduce the relevant contrasts. An attempt has therefore been made in what follows to take the average for a run of years close to the epidemic which did not contain fluctuations in mortality, and of course the same years have been taken for each parish. This should permit fair comparisons between parishes in a single epidemic year. But for the reasons Dr. Schofield gives, any comparison between different crisis years on the basis of these figures is more suspect, since rising or declining population trends may affect the relationship between the chosen 'average' and the exceptional year.
5. The chantry returns for Bristol are printed in E.E. Williams, *The Chantries of William Canynges in St. Mary Redcliffe Bristol,* 1950, Appendix pp. 32-41.
6. 'Two Bristol Calendars', p. 134; *Adams' Chronicle,* p. 178; Ricart, *Kalendar,* p. 59.
7. J.C. Russell, *British Medieval Population,* 1948, pp. 46,50; B.Little, *The City and County of Bristol,* 1954, p. 325; J. Latimer, *Annals of Bristol in the Seventeenth Century,* 1900, p.34.
8. B.A.O., Mayors' Audits 1624-5, p. 45, 1625-6, pp. 97, 165; Common Council Proceedings 1608-27, ff. 128v, 134v, 1627-42, ff. 25, 69r, 70v, 77r.
9. B.A.O., Mayors' Audits 1624-5, p.35; Temple Wardens' Accounts 1625, 1626. The billeting of troops in Bristol may partly account for disease in the town in 1628: Common Council Proceedings 1627-42, f.6r.

10. *Ibid.,* f. 84r; Temple Wardens' Accounts 1637; St. Mary Redcliffe Church, Church-wardens' Accounts, May 1637.

11. B.A.O., Mayors' Audits 1640-1, pp. 109-11; 1641-2, pp. 161-3; 1642-3, p. 243; Common Council Proceedings 1627-42, f. 123v.

12. *The Tragedy of the Kings Armies Fidelity since their entring into Bristol,* 1643, p. 6. Cf. E. Greaves, *Morbus Epidemius Anni 1643 or the New Disease,* 1643, pp. 11-12.

13. Cf. Clarendon, *History of the Rebellion,* ed. Macray, iv. 47; (Anon.) *The Sieges of Bristol during the Civil War,* 1868. The parish registers of All Saints, St. Stephen's and Temple all referred to 'plague' in 1645; they had not done so in 1643.

14. PRO E 179/247/6, E 179/113/192.

15. Cf. *The Inhabitants of Bristol in 1696,* ed. E. Ralph and M.E. Williams (Bristol Record Soc., xxv, 1968), p. xxiv.

16. CF. T.H. Hollingsworth, *Historical Demography,* 1969, p. 365; R. Pollitzer, *Plague,* 1954, pp. 486-7, 494-5.

17. *Bristol and its Adjoining Counties,* ed. C.M. MacInnes and W.F. Whittard, 1955, Map, p. 23; E.M. Carus-Wilson, *Medieval Merchant Venturers,* 2nd edn. 1967, p.4. I have been unable to see the register of St. Thomas's parish but each epidemic appears to have affected it severely: D.K. Gosling, 'The Parish Registers of the Churches of SS. Philip and Jacob and S. Thomas in Bristol' (Bristol Univ. M.A. thesis 1934), p.65.

18. *The Inhabitants of Bristol in 1696,* p. xii; Carus-Wilson, *Medieval Merchant Venturers,* p. 75; *Antiquities of Bristow in the Middle Centuries,* ed. J. Dallaway, 1834, p. 145. Cf. the large sums spent annually on the poor in St. Mary Redcliffe: St. Mary Redcliffe Church, Churchwardens' Accounts 1588-98 *passim;* B.A.O., Quarter Sessions Book 1642-3, f. 201r.

19. Cf. Pollitzer, *Plague,* pp. 578-80; L.F. Hirst, *The Conquest of Plague,* 1953, pp. 294-5.

20. W. Camden, *Britannia,* ed. E. Gibson, 1722, i. 94. Cf. Carus-Wilson, *Medieval Merchant Venturers,* p. 11; Ricart, *Kalendar,* p. 47.

21. B.A.O., Grand Jury Presentments 1628-66, 28 April 1629 and *passim.*

22. B.A.O., Easter Books of Christ Church Central. All communicants were expected to contribute and the collectors listed their names household by household along each street. But it is not always possible to tell at which end of the street they began, nor in the case of the Pithay and Tower Lane, on which side.

23. B.A.O., Mayors' Audits, 1595-6; *Adams' Chronicle,* pp. 149, 153.

24. It is surprising that there was no rise in the number of burials in St. James's Parish, but the register appears to be defective in 1597-9.

25. On the possibility of typhus spreading beyond the poor once it has become epidemic, see W.P. MacArthur, 'The Medical History of the Famine' in *The Great Famine,* ed. R.D. Edwards and T.D. Williams, 1956, pp. 278-80.

26. J.D. Chambers, *Population, Economy and Society in Pre-industrial England,* 1972, ch. 4.

27. The shortage of corn in Bristol at the end of 1550 is mentioned in B.L.Lansdowne MS. 2, f. 91.

28. Over the period 1605-39 there were 169 baptisms for every 100 burials in St. Nicholas's parish and 119 in St. Mary Redcliffe, for example.

29. Cf. B.A.O., Common Council Proceedings 1608-27, f. 124v; Quarter Sessions Book 1620-9, f. 76v.

30. E.g. in Norwich. W. Rye, *Depositions taken before the Mayor and Aldermen of Norwich 1549-67,* 1905, p. 70.

31. See my forthcoming book, *The Impact of Plague in Tudor and Stuart England*.
32. *Adams' Chronicle,* pp. 178, 216-7; S. Seyer, *Memoirs Historical and Topographical of Bristol,* 1821-3, i. 274-5.

The Most Famous Of All English Plagues

A detailed analysis of the Plague at Eyam, 1665-6

Leslie Bradley

Introduction

In his *History of Epidemics in Britain,*[1] Charles Creighton described the outbreak of plague at Eyam as 'the most famous of all English plagues: the story of it has been told many times in prose and verse, the moral incidents being well suited to minor poets and moral writers, and the whole of the drama conveniently centred within a circuit of half a mile in a cup of the healthy hills'. His own account, taken lock, stock and barrel from Wood's *The History and Antiquities of Eyam* (1842) adds nothing but some erroneous reflections on the epidemiology of the outbreak and his assertion that, however well intentioned, Mompesson's action in persuading the villagers to isolate themselves from the outside world was, in fact, a grim mistake. Nor, indeed, has any other writer added anything substantial to the story.

It is still less than a hundred years since the bacteriological causation of plague was discovered, and even now there are sharp differences of opinion on certain aspects of the disease.[2] It is not surprising, then, that there is controversy over the historical plagues. How great a mortality could they cause? What was the age and sex incidence of the mortality? What flea was responsible for the transmission of the disease? Why did plague die out in England after 1671? It may well be that a series of case studies might help to resolve some of these issues. Eyam would seem to afford an opportunity for such a study, but clearly it must be based on contemporary documents rather than on a fallible oral tradition recorded in print almost two centuries after the event.

The object of this essay, then, is to attempt such a detailed study, not only in order to compare the results of the analysis with the oral tradition on which Wood relied, but as a contribution to what it is hoped may be a continuing attempt to use local studies to illuminate the controversies mentioned in the last paragraph.

An account of the sources used and of the methods of analysis will be found as appendices. The Table and Figures will be found grouped at the end of the essay.

The Existing Literature

Apart from a brief account by Dr. Richard Mead in *A Discourse on the Plague* (1744) and an even shorter mention by Dr. Thomas Short in *A General Chronological History of the Air* (1749), both reprinted in Appendix I, I have not been able to trace any account of the Eyam plague until the last decade of the eighteenth century, some 130 years after the actual occurrence, when William Seward published some of Mompesson's letters and Anne Seward wrote accounts based in the main upon oral tradition. Several others followed, all mainly concerned with the dreadful extent of the devastation caused by the plague, the heroism of the villagers and the inspired leadership of Mompesson. All were surpassed by the publication in 1842 of Wood's *History and Antiquities of Eyam,* a large part of which is devoted to the story of the plague. Wood's sources were the parish registers and the oral tradition which, living himself in Eyam, he had sedulously collected. This has been the basis for the many versions which have appeared in a variety of books on Derbyshire; and the more scholarly works which have appeared more recently have, for the most part, accepted it uncritically. Creighton's *History of Epidemics in Britain* has already been mentioned. G.R. Batho[3] corrects the faulty epidemiology of Creighton, substituting that of Hirst[4] and throwing justified doubt on Wood's estimate of the population of Eyam, but he adds nothing substantial by way of analysis. Professor J.F.D. Shrewsbury[5] uses Wood's account to support his own Hirstian epidemiology of plague and his views on the extent of the mortality which plague could cause, but again adds nothing of importance.

Wood's Account of the Plague

Writing at a time when descriptions of the Lake District mountains and even of some of the Derbyshire heights were written in terms more appropriate to the Matterhorn, Wood's account is couched in the most florid and romantic language. Parts of it are of the nature of a romantic novel rather than a history, for he recounts thoughts and conversations of which he can have had no knowledge, even from tradition. His work ran into eight editions, the last in 1903, and it is interesting to find that by that time some of his earlier statements had been considerably modified. In the first edition, for example, Wood declares that 'It is a matter of fact that this terrible plague was brought to Eyam in a box of old clothes and some tailor's patterns of cloth.' By 1903 it was only 'most positively stated' and 'according to traditional accounts.' His detailed account of the course of the illness of the first victim becomes considerably less specific by the time it reaches the last edition, and the touching account of the parting of Mompesson and his wife from their children, first written as a factual account, is repeated in the last edition as being what 'imagination may paint.' Amusingly, a village housewife's 'snow-white bosom' becomes her 'sun-browned bosom'. Nevertheless, despite all his florid writing and fanciful imaginings, Wood's account does afford a good deal of factual information. Unfortunately, it is not easy to determine when, in any given statement, he is making an inference from information gleaned from the parish register and when he is relying on oral tradition. As might be expected, after a lapse of some 176 years, the oral tradition, however interesting and useful, was not entirely reliable and events are described which are not in accord with the known nature of plague.

Wood describes the arrival at Eyam, on September 2nd or 3rd, 1665, of a box sent from London to a tailor in Eyam and containing clothing and samples. On opening this, George Vicars almost immediately became ill and developed swellings in the neck and groin. The 'fatal token - the plague spot - appeared on his breast' and he died on September 6th. A second victim, living in the same house, followed a fortnight later. By the end of September six persons had died and others followed rapidly, twenty-two dying in October. The disease slackened in intensity during November but, despite a hard winter which normally puts an end to a plague epidemic, deaths continued on a reduced scale until May 1666. In June the disease burst out again with renewed vigour. The Rector, William Mompesson, sent his two children away, and other inhabitants had left the village. 'The most wealthy of them, who were but few in number', says Wood, 'had fled early in the Spring. Some few others, having means, fled to the neighbouring hills and there erected huts and dwelled therein until the approach of winter.' But Mompesson, fearing that fleeing inhabitants would carry 'the invisible seeds of the disease' in their clothing and so spread the infection, persuaded the remaining inhabitants of the village to confine themselves within a circle of about half a mile around the village. At two or three points on this boundary provisions were brought from adjoining villages and later collected by Eyam villagers. Many of the necessities were provided, it is said, by the Earl of Devonshire free of charge, but where money was needed it was deposited in springs or troughs of running water. Towards the end of June the church and churchyard were closed. Services were held in the open in the Delf, the congregation sitting spread over a hillside, and burial had to be in fields and gardens, without the funeral rites. There were twenty-one deaths in June, fifty-five in July and seventy-six in August, one of them Mompesson's wife. The houses from the eastern end to the middle of the village, says Wood, were now nearly empty. The inhabitants of the extreme western end of the village, who were at that time very few, shut themselves up in their houses and would not cross a small stream dividing them from the rest of the village. The plague now began to subside and 'on the eleventh of October, 1666, after having from the first day of the same month destroyed fifteen out of forty-five, totally ceased. After having swept away five-sixths of the inhabitants of Eyam, this the greatest enemy of the human race was exhausted with excessive slaughter, and in the last conflict worsted and destroyed and buried with its last victim.'

Wood quotes a letter from Mompesson in which he states that seventy-six families were visited by the plague and 259 persons died, the last on October 11th. He asserts that the population at the beginning of the calamity 'has generally been stated at 330, but from the number of families visited by the plague, mentioned in the subsequent letter of Mompesson, it would, I opine, be nearer the mark to say 350, or perhaps a few more.' 'Of all the devastating traces of the destructive malady,' he writes, 'there is none which to the present day has been more generally talked of than that the main street from one end of the village to the other, was grown over with grass; and, it is said, kingcups and other flowers grew in the very middle of the road.' He adds the stories of some of the families which suffered most severely, the Mortens and Kemps of Shepherds Flatt, the Hancocks and Talbots of Riley.

The Parish and Village of Eyam

First, however, it might be useful to describe the locality in which the events of 1665-6 occurred. The parish of Eyam, situated in the Derbyshire hills, some ten miles south west of Sheffield and on the eastern edge of the Peak District, comprises some 3,000 acres. The main settlement is the village of Eyam, with smaller settlements at Foolow, two miles from Eyam, and Grindleford Bridge, just over a mile and a half from Eyam. There are, in addition, a number of small groups of farm houses and isolated farms.

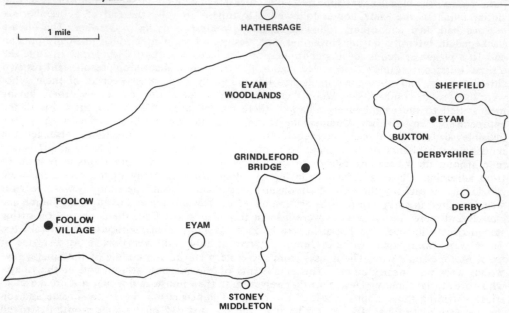

There is some confusion in Wood between the parish and the village. When he says that five-sixths of the inhabitants died of plague he is almost certainly referring to the village, though in his statistics he appears to have included burials of persons who lived in the parish but not even in the township. His estimate of a population of 350 cannot have been even approximately accurate for the whole parish, as will appear later.

It was a parish of small farms and leadmines, with few big houses. The 1662 Hearth Tax return lists only eight houses as having more than two hearths and six as having two, the remaining 112 having only one. And these are only the charged houses; those not liable to tax would not be large houses. It is relevant to mention that the majority of houses in Eyam at this date are likely to have been constructed of stone, with earth or stone floors and roofed with stone slabs[6].

The small village of Stoney Middleton, a mile to the south of Eyam, was part of the parish of Hathersage, whose parish church lies some four miles north of Stoney Middleton and on the other side of Eyam parish. It would appear from the Eyam parish register that between 1645 and 1670 a number of Middleton families were in the habit of baptising their children at Eyam instead of making the long journey to Hathersage, but this does not appear to have been the case with burials.

The Population of Eyam

Confusion is likely to arise between the population of the whole parish of Eyam and that of the village of Eyam. Wood, for example, estimates the population as 350 and this can only refer to the village, or at the most to the township. Yet the total which he gives of plague deaths includes the whole parish, and his descriptions of the families which suffered most grievously include some which were certainly 'outlying'.

It is notoriously difficult to make firm estimates of population at this period. We might expect to have three methods available, using the parish registers, the Hearth Tax returns and, for a slightly later date, the Compton Census. Unfortunately, the 1664 Hearth Tax return is incomplete and cannot be used for this purpose, whilst the 1662 and 1667 returns, omitting 'uncharged' houses, do not provide adequate information.

The use of parish registers to estimate population depends on making assumptions about the birth and death rates prevailing at the appropriate period. If, for example, a reasonable annual average of births in a given parish were sixty and we knew the birth rate to be thirty per thousand, then the population would be approximately 2,000. In fact, of course, we do not know the birth rate. It varied from parish to parish and from time to time within the parish, and this was long before the time when adequate statistical records were kept. Birth rates as high as fifty per thousand and as low as twenty-five per thousand undoubtedly occurred, but these are extremes and it would be reasonable to assume, for Eyam, a birth rate of between thirty and forty per thousand. A further complication is that parish registers do not indicate the number of births, but only of baptisms and there is little doubt that not all births were recorded as baptisms. Table 1 shows that, in 1660, the annual number of baptisms was around thirty-three. At thirty per thousand this would give an estimated population for the parish of 1,100 and at forty per thousand of 825, and to these should be added some allowance for under-registration.

The same kind of argument applies to death rates. As the number of burials is, on the average, less than the number of baptisms in Eyam at this time, it would appear that the death rate was probably lower than the birth rate. Taking limits of twenty-five and thirty-five per thousand, and the annual average of burials as twenty-seven, we have a population estimate for the parish of between 1,080 and 771 to which should be added, as before, an allowance for under-registration.

The Compton Census was an ecclesiastical return, made in 1676, in which the incumbent was required, in effect, to state the number of persons in his parish who were of communicant age. The return for Eyam was 532 and though Batho[3] states that this was for the township, it must surely have been, as in other places, for the whole parish. It is usually, though not with certainty, estimated that those of communicant age represented sixty per cent of the total population, which would give an estimate for the whole parish ten years after the plague of 887.

Finally, Tables II, IV and V show that the parish contained at least 246 families, and this would suggest a total population in the neighbourhood of 1,000. It is reasonable to conclude that it is unlikely that the population of the parish was less than 850 and that it might well have been 1,000 or even more.

What proportion of this total population can be attributed to the township of Eyam is difficult to estimate. The 1662 Hearth Tax return indicated 48 charged houses for Eyam, 43 for Foolow and 26 for Woodlands, but uncharged houses are not included and are likely to have been a larger proportion of the whole in the township than in the smaller hamlets. Indeed, from the incomplete 1664 return, the township may have had more uncharged than charged houses. Pilkington, in 1788, made a survey of Derbyshire, counting or estimating the number of houses in each parish and, in some cases, stating his estimate of the population. His figures for Eyam are:

	Houses	Inhabitants
Eyam township	180	918
Foolow and Grindlow	94	
Woodlands	40	
Grindleford	24	

This gives the township an average of 5.1 persons per house. One would expect a lower rate for the farming areas, and if we take the more usual rate of 4.5 per house in the farming areas, we arrive at a total population for the parish of some 1,600 of whom 56% are attributable to the township. If we assume, as seems likely, that the township grew faster than the outlying areas, we would expect the township in 1660 to contribute less than 56% of the parish total. Even on our minimum estimate of 850 for the parish population. Wood's figure of 350 would appear too low for the township, being only 40% of the total, and it would certainly be too low if the parish population approached 1,000. On the other hand, at our minimum estimate it might well be a reasonable estimate for the actual village, though probably too low if the total population approached 1,000.

The register and the Hearth Tax returns afford us some information as to the geographical distribution of the families which are the subject of this study. The boundaries of the Hearth Tax areas, Eyam township, Foolow and Woodlands are not definitely established. The parish register frequently indicates residence outside the township (as, for example, 'Foolow', 'Bridge', 'Brosterfield'), though there is evidence that it sometimes fails to do so. It has been possible to arrive at three groups:

a. those families indicated by the register or Hearth Tax as living in the 'outlying' areas, Foolow or Woodlands.

b. those families indicated by Hearth Tax as being in the township, though it is impossible to tell whether they actually lived in the village.

c. those for whom there is no such indication. So far as Hearth Tax is concerned, this may either be because they did not pay tax or because, as indicated above, parts of the return are illegible. Since, however, the register so frequently specifies the 'outliers', it seems likely that the majority of these 'unknown' cases belonged to the township. In Tables II, IV and VII the distribution of the families concerned between these three groups has been shown.

The Origin of the Eyam Plague

We have seen that Wood describes how a box containing patterns and clothes from London, where plague was raging, arrived at Eyam on September 2nd or 3rd. It was unpacked by George Vicars who, observing that they were damp, hung them before the fire to dry. He was suddenly seized with violent sickness and other symptoms, grew horribly worse on the second day, was delirious and showed large swellings on his neck and groin. On the third day, the plague spot appeared on his breast and he died on September 6th. This story of the origin of the Eyam plague, possibly elaborated from the account by Mead quoted in the Appendix, has been accepted by all subsequent writers, but it raises considerable difficulties. The noticeable feature is the rapidity of the onset of the disease. This is characteristic of pneumonic plague and of the septicaemic form of bubonic plague. But pneumonic plague is unlikely in view of its highly infectious character and the slow development of the Eyam epidemic, the next victim dying a fortnight later. Moreover, buboes would not appear. Septicaemic plague, too, develops so rapidly that the typical plague symptoms would not have time to appear. The remaining alternative is a severe attack of normal bubonic plague, but the difficulty here is the very short incubation period, only a few hours. Such cases have been reported but they are extremely rare, and the average incubation period is reported as being of the order of three days.

Batho, indeed, suggests a possible alternative.[3] Wood describes how an unusual number of visitors arrived in Eyam to join in the merrymaking at the Eyam Wakes in 1665. Quoting Hutton,[7] Batho asserts that Derby was severely affected by plague in that year and suggests that a visitor from Derby may have brought with him an infected flea and so started the Eyam epidemic. Let us examine the possibility.

According to Wood, the Eyam Wakes took place on the first Sunday after August 18th. This would be August 20th, thirteen or fourteen days before Vicars fell ill and seventeen days before his death. Investigations reported by Pollitzer[8] suggest a period of between two and five days, according to the severity of the infection, between a rat becoming infected by a plague-infected flea and the rat dying, whilst Wu Lien-Teh[9] suggests that three days will elapse before the fleas from the dead rat are ready to attack man, followed by an incubation period of three days for the human plague to develop and an average illness period of five and a half days before death. If a rat flea brought to the Wakes were the source of infection, this would fit nicely into the period between the Wakes and Vicars' death. If, on the other hand, a human flea were responsible for the transmission of the plague from the visitor to Vicars one would expect the period to be shorter.

Batho adds: 'the traditional explanation of the coming of the plague to Eyam is, however, the more probable.' It is difficult to see why, having accepted the Derby epidemic, he should so conclude! But was there plague in Derby in 1665? Hutton is quite explicit: '1665. Derby was again visited by the plague at the same time in which London fell under the same calamity. The town was forsaken: the farmers declined the market place and grass grew upon the spot which had furnished the support of life...' The Victoria County History of Derbyshire also mentions a violent outbreak of plague in Derby in 1665, though its authority appears to be Hutton. Shrewsbury complicates the issue by placing the Derby outbreak in 1666 and quotes Bell[10] 'The town of Derby suffered severly in 1666. The residents, with Eyam's example before them, mostly fled...' This statement certainly appears in the first edition of Bell but has disappeared in the second edition, which says that 'Derbyshire, apart from the village of Eyam, was immune.' And my examination of the registers of the Derby parishes reveals no excessive mortality, nothing which could suggest any epidemic outbreak in either 1665 or 1666.

How plague came to Eyam must, then, remain in doubt.

The Progress of the Plague

Figure 3, exhibiting the weekly totals of burials in 1665 and 1666, shows the onset of increased mortality in September 1665; a peak in October; continuing, though lower, mortality throughout the winter and spring; a steep rise in burials in June 1666; the high peak of thirty-one burials at the end of July and the beginning of August; and the termination of the epidemic in October.

Not all of these burials were due to plague. The register does not give the cause of death and, even during the plague period, other diseases would continue to take their toll. Indeed, examination of the reconstitution forms reveals at least six cases where the death of an infant was most unlikely to have been due to plague, this burial being, in some cases the only one suffered by the family in the plague period. One would expect, too, some deaths from respiratory diseases amongst old people during the winter months.

The distribution of burials in the summer of 1666 shows all the characteristics of a plague epidemic, as does, in a small way, that of October 1665, but further discussion is needed of the persistence of the epidemic through the winter. Shrewsbury repeatedly asserts that, of its very nature, plague would only persist in a mild winter and that many winter epidemics which have been attributed to plague were, in fact, due to other diseases such as influenza and typhus.[11] Though others have disputed this assertion, it is generally agreed that the cold winter months are unfavourable to plague. Wood, in his first edition, says that 'In December, a great snow is said to have fallen, with a hard and severe frost...The weather at the commencement of 1666 was exceedingly cold and severe', though these assertions have disappeared by his final edition. Thomas Short, a Sheffield physician who made a study of the effects of weather on disease, makes no mention of this hard winter.[12] The following figures are relevant.

Table X   Winter month burials.

	Nov.	Dec.	Jan.	Feb.	Mar.	Apl.	May.	Total
1665–6	6	10	4	8	6	9	4	47
Annual average								
1631-40	2.5	1.7	2.4	2.0	2.3	2.4	2.5	
1641-50	1.8	1.7	1.9	1.8	2.4	2.3	2.8	
1651-60	0.9	2.5	2.1	1.8	2.8	3.2	2.5	
1661-64	1.3	2.5	1.8	1.8	3.5	3.0	3.0	
Highest Recorded for that month excluding 1665-6	5	7	8	7	8	7	7	
Occuring in	1636 1639 1668	1680	1676	1682	1651	1651 1662	1673	

It will be seen that in none of these winter and spring months of 1665-6, considered separately, was the mortality much higher than previous peaks, but that the mortality persisted throughout these months instead of being confined to one or two months. The total number of burials from November 1665 to May 1666 inclusive was forty-seven; the previous highest totals for the same months were twenty-six in 1639-40 and in 1650-51. All this makes it appear that some epidemic was in progress throughout the winter, and the fact that no previous winter had produced mortality on this scale appears to lend some support to the suggestion that the plague epidemic of September and October continued on a smaller scale throughout the winter and recrudesced in June 1666. However, when we examine the forty-seven deaths there is no clear evidence of the persistence of plague. Three deaths in one family occurred in early November, very possibly the last victims of the 1665 plague outbreak; eighteen deaths in seventeen families give no sign of the infection being passed on inside the family; one death is in the Hawkesworth family which, as explained on page 72 is so confused as to have to be excluded; only the following six cases need further consideration:

Rowland: Nov 5th, Dec 1st, Jan 15th, Feb 14th.
Rowbotham: Dec 9th, Dec 24th, Jan 1st (2 deaths)
Rowe: Dec 14th, Dec 15th, Dec 19th.
Blackwall: Dec 24th, Feb 21st, Mar 2nd, Apl 6th, Apl 16th.
Wilson: Dec 22nd, Jan 28th, Feb 15th, Feb 17th, Feb 18th, Mar 1st.
Thorpe: Apl 15th, Apl 30th (2 deaths).

Of these, only three, Rowbotham, Rowe and Thorpe look anything like the intra-familial plague pattern, the Thorpes being possibly the first victims, of the 1666 outbreak. The intervals between burials in the other cases are longer than one would expect in the same family if all were due to plague.

When did the plague epidemic end? In a letter dated November 20th, 1666, Mompesson writes that 'none have died of the plague since October 11th.' This raises a difficulty. The late September and the October burials recorded in the register are:

Sept 20th.   Francis Morten de Foolow
     21st.   George ye son of Samuel Butterworth
     22nd   Anne ye wife of Francis Torre de Bretton
     23rd.   1. Anne ye wife of Joseph Glover predict
              2. Anne ye wife of Peter Hall defunct
              3. Francis ye son of Anne Hawkesworth wid
     29th.   1. An infant of ye above said Fra: Townend
              2. Susanna ye daughter of Francis Morten defunct
Oct 1st.   Jonas Parsley
     2nd.   Grace ye wife of Francis Morten defunct
     4th.   Peter ye son of Thomas Ash defunct
     5th.   Abraham ye son of Francis Morten defunct
     -        1. Thomas Torre senior   (Oct 6th)*
     -        2. Benjamin ye son of Fra: Morten defunct
     -        1. Elizabeth ye daughter of ye said Fra: Morten   (Oct 8th)
     -        2. Alice ye daughter of Alice Teylour predict
     -        Anne ye wife of Jonas Parsley defunct   (Oct 11th)
     -        Agnes ye daughter of Thomas and Agnes Sheldon   (Oct 11th)

71

-	Mary the daughter of Francis Morten defunct	(Oct 12th)
-	Samuel and Peter sons of Peter Hall defunct	(Oct 13th)
-	Joseph ye son of Francis Morten	(Oct 14th)
15th	Grace ye daughter of ye said Fra:	
17th	1. Elizabeth ye wife of John Danyell defunct	
	2. Anne ye daughter of John Grundy de Foolow	
18th	Francis ye son of Fra: Morten above said	
28th	William ye son of ye said Fra: Morten	

*Dates in brackets come from the Bishops Transcripts

This sequence in no way differs from those of earlier months and, especially in view of the mortality in the Morten family, the possibility that these were still plague deaths must be kept in mind. Even the ten day gap before the death of William Morten is not inconsistent with plague, for he is over the age of twenty and could have been away in service, returning home when, in the middle of October, his younger brothers and sisters were in difficulties after the deaths of their parents. I have, therefore, defined the plague period as being from September 7th 1665, the date of the burial of the first victim, George Vicars, to the end of October 1666, so that I take into account nine burials occurring after Mompesson's terminal date.

It must be emphasised that the statistical Tables in this study relate to the whole of the burials, irrespective of the cause of death, occurring in the plague period as I have defined it above.

The Degree of Mortality and its Geographical, Age and Sex Incidence

Table II analyses all the families for which burials are recorded in the plague period, Four sets had to be rejected from the analysis:

Christopher Chapman:	difficulty over the status of the only member of the family buried during this period.
John Hadfield:	three or possibly four families which could not be disentangled.
Peter Hawkesworth:	two or possibly three families entangled.
Adam Hawkesworth:	two or possibly three families entangled.

In all, then, between eight and eleven families were excluded, the evidence suggesting that not more than five of these suffered burials in the plague period. The remaining eighty-nine families were then analysed according to the effects of the burials on the heads of families, and an attempt was made, as described earlier, to investigate their geographical distribution. Single individuals, sixteen in number, who could not be ascribed to a family but who died in the plague period were not included in the analysis.

According to Mompesson's letter of November 20th, 1666, 'There have been seventy-six families visited within my parish, out of whom 259 persons died.' Wood, taking the burial of Joseph Morten as the final one due to plague, counts 267 burials and ascribes the difference to the possibility that Mompesson had disregarded deaths which he knew were not due to plague. My count, including all burials to the end of October, is 276.

There is an apparent discrepancy in the number of families attacked. Table II shows eighty-nine families involved, in addition to sixteen individuals who could not be ascribed to families, whereas Mompesson's figure of families attacked by plague is seventy-six. The discrepancy is reduced by three considerations:

1. that some of the unascribed individuals would be living in families - a widowed mother, for example, might be living with a son's family.
2. that Mompesson may have disregarded families in which the only burials were not attributable to plague.
3. that if two 'families', in the restricted sense of husband, wife and their children, lived in the same house, forming one household, Mompesson could well have counted them as one family.

The actual discrepancy seems likely to be small.

Geographical Distribution

Table II shows that at least forty-eight of the burials were of families from the outlying areas, Foolow and Woodlands, 150 from Eyam township and seventy-eight unattributed. At the worst, then, 228 burials could be attributed to the township.

Age and sex distribution

Table VIII distributes the burials in each month of the plague period according to sex and apparent age (that is, the interval between baptism and burial).

Looking at the percentage of the total burials falling on each age group, the most striking feature of the plague period is the greatly increased proportional mortality (over three times that of the previous fourteen years) falling on the age group five to nineteen years, as contrasted with the slightly reduced proportion in the age group one to four years and the very greatly reduced share of those under the age of one year. Those over twenty years made roughly the same contribution, though it must be remembered that we have no means of breaking this group down into smaller sub-groups between which there might have been significant differences.

So far as they go, then, our figures agree with Hirst who says that the majority of bubonic cases occur in persons between ten and thirty-five years of age, the very young and the very old being little affected,[13] and with Pollitzer who assigns the highest incidence to adolescents and adults up to the age of forty-five,[14] as well as with a study by M.F. and T.H. Hollingsworth of a London parish in the first quarter of the seventeenth century, where they found that in plague periods the percentage of burials attributed to the age groups up to four years and over forty-five years decreased, whilst those between four and forty-four years increased.[15]

There was no great difference between the total mortality of males and females, and this again agrees with Hirst and Pollitzer.

The Demographic Effects

The parish as a whole

Reference to Table I shows that, over the three decades prior to the plague, burial averages fluctuated between twenty and twenty-six per annum and were slightly higher in the two decades following the plague. If we adopt Dr. Schofield's admittedly arbitrary definition of a year of crisis mortality as being one in which the number of burials exceeds double an appropriate average,[16] there are no crisis years between 1631 and 1690 other than the plague years and there are only four, 1642, 1657, 1675 and 1682 in which the mortality was fifty per cent above either the moving average or the decadal average. Apart from the plague years, then, in spite of fluctuating mortality, Eyam had suffered no severe crisis of mortality.

Baptism averages tended to rise slowly between 1631 and 1660 and the number of baptisms rose quite sharply in 1663 and 1664. They were heavily depressed in 1666 but recovered in 1667 and reached a peak in 1668, and the decade 1661-70, though it contained the plague period, actually produced the highest total of baptisms in the period under review. A brief relapse followed between 1673 and 1676, but it was not until after 1680 that the rate of baptisms began effectively to fall below the pre-plague level.

Marriages, too, had begun to increase before the plague, were depressed in 1666 but recovered in 1667 and reached a peak in 1668. Once again, the decade 1661-70 produced the highest total of marriages in the whole period, and the two decades following the plague contributed more marriages than the two which had preceded the plague decade.

Turning now to the Cumulative Natural Increase (Table I and figure 2)., it will be seen that 1665 and 1666 wiped out the whole of the Natural Increase which had been built up since 1631. But recovery began immediately, without the period of stagnation which has been observed in some case studies, and the rate of increase was, until 1673, even more rapid than the rate in the pre-plague years. A minor setback occurred in 1674 and 1675 and thereafter the rate of increase became slower. It must be remembered, of course, that the Cumulative Natural Increase does not indicate the actual population increase, since it takes no account of migration into or out of the parish, but it has been found to give a useful picture of the demographic fortunes of the parish concerned.

Consideration of these facts, with especial attention to the years immediately following 1666, does not, in spite of the heavy plague mortality, convey the impression of a 'devastated' parish. Recovery was, in fact, quite rapid. Some impression of how this recovery occurred can be gained by using our reconstitution to study individual families.

Table II analyses eighty-nine families with recorded burials in the plague period. Table IV concerns families which can be shown to exist in the parish, either by register entries or Hearth Tax returns, between 1660 and 1665 and for which no plague period deaths are recorded. Again, single unascribed individuals have been excluded, as have those for whom the only record is a marriage with not more than one baptism. This latter exclusion eliminates marriages where the groom is from outside the parish, allowing for the not uncommon custom of bring the first child for baptism in the mother's parish of origin. It may, of course, also eliminate a small number of genuine Eyam marriages, but the error is in the right direction. This leaves us with 157 families. Of the 246 families, then, whose existence during or immediately before the plague can be established, 157 escaped the plague, that is nearly sixty-four per cent.

Of the eighty-nine families suffering plague-period burials, seventeen became extinct, so far as our records show, and a further thirty-six show no further record either in the register or in Hearth Tax returns. Of the 157 families not suffering plague-period burials, twenty-one show no record between 1666 and 1690. Table V, then, suggests that 172 families are known or are likely to have remained in existence after the plague, that is some seventy per cent of those existing immediately before the plague.

The distribution of the plague-period burials as between families is shown in Table III. It will be seen that well over a quarter of the families suffered only one burial and a further quarter only two, though this ignores the sixteen non-ascribed individuals, some of whom may have been residing in affected families.

Thus it would seem that sufficient families remained in existence to account for the rapid post-plague revival and this is borne out by analyses of the baptisms between 1667 and 1670 and of the nature of the new families arising in the ten years after the plague.

Table VI records 'new' families, that is families in which the head did not appear in the register as marrying or as a father before 1667. In some cases he can be identified with reasonable certainty as a child of a pre-plague Eyam family; in others he has the same surname as a pre-plague family or group of families and the circumstances suggest that he sprang from it; in yet others there appears to be no connection with a pre-plague family. Here again, marriages with not more than one baptism have been excluded. Of the seventy new families recorded between 1666 and 1676, no less than fifty-seven were probably related to pre-plague families and only thirteen appear to be entirely new to the parish.

Similarly, Table VII shows that in 1667 and 1668 the majority of baptisms were to families in existence before the plague. There is no means of knowing how far the high figure of baptisms in the immediate post-plague years is due to the baptism of children born in the plague period but whose baptisms were postponed. Did the inhabitants of Eyam avoid having children during the plague period or did births proceed normally with baptisms postponed? Even if we assume, say, a rate of thirty-five baptisms per annum for 1665 and 1666, the shortfall is no more than seventy less the number of baptisms recorded in those years, namely thirty-four and sixteen, leaving an actual shortfall of twenty and there are still 159 baptisms to be accounted for to the end of 1670, an average of nearly forty per annum.

The evidence suggests, then, that the effects of the plague on the parish as a whole were not so disastrous as to prevent it from re-establishing itself demographically in quite a short time and without heavy immigration of families from outside.

As has been pointed out, Wood's assertion that the plague 'swept away five sixths of the inhabitants of Eyam' refers to the village and not to the whole parish. Unfortunately we cannot, from our sources, effectively separate events in the village from those in the township. Nine deaths in the plague period are attributed to Shepherds Flatt and fourteen to Riley, both outside the village but within the township, but we have no means of knowing what relation the population of the village bore to that of the township. In view of the scattered nature of habitations outside the village it seems likely that the great majority of the inhabitants of the township actually lived in the village, but in default of precise ascriptions of residence we can only, in this study, make estimates for the whole township.

Table II shows seventy-eight burials described as 'situation unknown'. We might distribute these according to a number of assumptions:

a. We can ascribe all the 'unknown' burials to the township, giving 228 township and 48 outlying burials. This gives the maximum number of registered burials which can be attributed to the township.

b. We can ascribe all the 'unknown' burials to the outlying areas, giving 150 township and 126 outlying burials. This gives the minimum number of burials which can be attributed to the township.

c. As an intermediate assumption, we can divide the 'unknown' burials in the ratio of the known burials, i.e. in the ratio 150 to 48. This gives 209 township and 67 outlying burials.

On page 67 it was suggested that the total population of the parish must have been at least 850 and that the maximum share attributable to the township was 56%. which would give a township population of 476 and an outlying population of 374. The percentage of the population dying in the township and in the outlying areas on the above three assumptions would then be:

		Township	Outlying
A1	a	47.9%	12.8%
	b	31.5%	33.7%
	c	43.9%	17.9%

On the assumption that, in 1666, the township accounted for no more than half the total minimum population, that is 425, the percentages would be:

		Township	Outlying
A2	a	53.6%	11.3%
	b	35.3%	29.6%
	c	49.2%	15.8%

Assumption b can be rejected, not only because it is inherently implausible but because it leads to the very unlikely conclusion that the percentage dying in the outlying areas was roughly the same as in the township. The other two assumptions give percentages dying ranging between 44% and 54% for the township and between 11% and 18% for the outlying areas. This, it must be emphasised, is using the minimum estimate for the parish population. If we assume a parish population of 1,000, the corresponding percentages are:

		Township	Outlying
B1	a	40.7%	10.9%
	c	37.3%	15.2%
B2	a	45.6%	9.6%
	c	41.8%	13.4%

giving percentages dying ranging between 37% and 46% for the township and between 9% and 15% for the outlying districts.

It seems likely, then, even allowing for under-registration, that the township lost no more than half of its original population, and probably less, and this comes nearer to the sort of maximum mortality quoted by modern authorities for plague epidemics. It is worth recalling, too, that Thomas Short, writing nearly a century before Wood, puts the mortality as 'near half of the village.'[17]

To return to Wood, the maximum number of deaths which could be attributed to the township was 228. Subtracting the twenty-three deaths at Shepherds Flatt and Riley, the maximum attributable to the village is 205. If this were five-sixths of the initial population, that population would be 246, so much below Wood's own estimate that even under-registration of burials could hardly account for the difference.

What of Wood's other statement that 'on the eleventh day of October 1666 this aweful minister of death, after having from the first day of the same month destroyed fourteen out of about forty-five and having carried away full five-sixths of the inhabitants of the village was exhausted with excessive slaughter and in its last conflict worsted and destroyed.' If thirty-one survivors were one-sixth of the initial population we have an initial population of around 180. Nor can we resolve these large discrepancies by assuming that Wood's five-sixths referred not to the original population but to those remaining after some had fled for, by his own account, these were few. 'The most wealthy of them, who were but few in number, fled early in the spring with the greatest precipitation. Some few others, having means, fled to the neighbouring hills and dells and there erected huts where they remained until the approach of winter.'

We may, then, conclude that the mortality, though heavy, was not as devastating as Wood suggests. At least ten of the twenty-seven baptisms (i.e. 37%) to pre-plague families which were registered in 1667 could be attributed to the township and at least fifteen of thirty-five (43%) in 1668 which suggests that the township was showing a reasonable rate of recovery though, as might be expected, slower than that of the parish as a whole.

Burial Intervals within Families

The attempt to investigate the temporal sequence of burials within individual families was prompted by the possibility that studies of this kind might throw some light on the rival rat-flea and human flea theories of the transmission of human plague. On the rat-flea theory, Shrewsbury suggests that the interval between the first case in a family and the second would be about fourteen days and that there might then be a number of other cases within quite a short period.[18] So far it has not been possible to obtain from the proponents of the human-flea theory a similar timetable, but one would, I think, expect shorter intervals. On either theory there would be two complications; firstly that the incubation period of bubonic plague varies as between individual cases, so that Shrewsbury's fourteen days would not be precise, but would show a scatter of two or three days on either side; secondly that these might not be a single first case, but sometimes two or even more who received the infection at the same time from an outside source and could die within a few days of each other - a 'multiple' first case.

The actual investigation is complicated by a number of factors:
1. We cannot be sure that a given burial is due to plague.
2. Adult children who were out at service might contract plague and die away from home, but their burial will be recorded on our forms as though they had died whilst living at home.
3. Some of the single individuals who died of plague and have not been ascribed to families would, in fact, be living with families, so that our burial intervals for such families will be incomplete.
The results of this study must, therefore, be treated with great caution, the more so as the sample is small.

Examination of the reconstitution forms of the eighty-nine families with plague-period burials shows eight where it is unlikely that plague was involved and twenty-two cases where there was only one burial in the family. This leaves fifty-nine cases to be analysed, and for these the time-intervals between the first and second burial was recorded (Table IX column A and Figure 4A), with the proviso that burials on the same day were treated as a single burial.

It will be seen that the intervals fall into two main groups, one of one to four days, the other of ten to twelve days. There were six cases in which the interval was over thirty days. It seems clear that in these cases there was no direct connection between the deaths, and in the three cases where a third burial followed, the interval between the second and third burials was used in the Table.

The variability of the incubation period suggests that burials occurring even three or four days apart might be due to the same infective source, so that a second Table was drawn up in which the cases asterisked in Table IX column A were redistributed, the interval now being taken as between the first and the third case in the sequence. Thus
    Case 1 - 3 days - case 2 - 12 days - case 3
is now counted as a fifteen-day interval. The new distribution is shown in Table IX column B and Figure 4B. The tendency to group around the nine to twelve day interval is even more marked.

Examination of the cases comprised in eight to fifteen-day intervals, thirty in number, showed that thirteen produced one or more further burials within five days, seven produced further burials after intervals longer than five days and ten produced no further burials.

Conclusion

It remains to consider what bearing this study has on the controversial issues in the study of plague.

Perhaps the most important issue is the degree of mortality and of social and economic dislocation caused by plague epidemics. Some historians, for example, have suggested that the Black Death wiped out half of the total population of England and had disastrous economic effects. Shrewsbury, at the other extreme, suggests that no more than one twentieth of the population died. His argument is that plague is mainly an urban disease, that modern experience suggests that the urban mortality rate in a plague epidemic is unlikely to exceed fifty per cent and that four fifths of the population lived outside the towns in rural areas where the mortality would be much lower and which might, indeed, escape untouched. And since he is arguing from the intrinsic nature of bubonic plague this would be equally true in the seventeenth century. The high mortality rate in a village like Eyam would appear to contradict him. Unfortunately the Eyam experience is far from typical. Mompesson's action in persuading the villagers to isolate themselves actually provided favourable conditions for the spread of the epidemic within the village and made the conditions far more akin to those of urban rather than of rural plague[19] and, as we have seen, produced the sort of mortality rate which is associated with a severe urban epidemic. It is significant that, even this high mortality rate did not prevent a rapid recovery.

The age incidence of the mortality is consistent with recent findings and with the analysis made by the Hollingsworths which is mentioned on page 73. The sex incidence agrees with recent findings, but not with the Hollingsworths who found considerably greater male than female mortality.

The seasonal pattern of plague epidemic in this country is well established, with its peak of deaths in August or September. In Eyam, the 1666 outbreak conforms to this pattern, and though the 1665 outbreak occurred a month or so later, this is by no means uncommon. What would have been welcome would be clearer evidence on the persistence of the plague throughout the winter. Shrewsbury asserts categorically that human plague can persist only through exceptionally mild winters, though it may persist amongst the rats and reappear as a human disease when the weather becomes warm again. In Eyam, the occurrence of unusually high winter mortality without any clear sign of a plague pattern within the affected families leaves the issue in doubt.

Finally there is the dispute as to whether the flea responsible for transmitting the disease from man to man was one of the rat fleas or the human flea. We have seen that Shrewsbury, who argues for indirect transmission through the rat flea and the rat[18], suggests that this involves in most cases an interval of about fourteen days between the first case in a family and the second, and this is in reasonable agreement with the interval of ten to twelve days which emerges from the discussion on page 78. In the light of the prevalence of the human flea in the seventeenth century, one might expect direct transmission from one human to another to involve a shorter interval, but no clear statement on this issue has come to our notice from the proponents of the human flea theory. The structure of the Eyam cottages may have some bearing. Some authorities have ascribed the decline and disappearance of plague in England to the replacement of timber-framed houses with wattle-and-daub walls, thatched roofs and earth floors, all of which provide meeting places for rats, by brick or stone dwellings with tiled roofs and stone or plaster floors. If the majority of cottages in Eyam in 1665 were stone built, with stone-slab roofs and frequently with stone floors[6], these would be precisely the conditions which are said to offer the least favourable conditions for rats.

It would be absurd to expect that any single case study could resolve any of the controversial issues, but perhaps this study may help to demonstrate some of the possibilities and difficulties of a detailed local analysis of a plague situation.

APPENDIX I

From *A Discourse on the Plague* - Richard Mead - 1744 pp 149-151

"The Plague was likewise at Eham in the Peak of Derbyshire, being brought thither by means of a Box sent from London to a Taylor in that Village, containing some Materials relating to his Trade. There being several incidents in this latter instance that will not only serve to establish in particular the Precepts I have been giving, in relation to Goods, but likewise all the rest of the Directions, that have been set down, for stopping the Progress of the Plague from one Town to another: I shall finish this Chapter with a particular Relation of what passed in that Place. A Servant, who first opened the foresaid Box, complaining that the Goods were damp, was ordered to dry them at the Fire; but in doing it was seized with the Plague and died: the same misfortune extended to all the rest of the Family, except the Taylor's wife, who alone survived. From hence the Distemper spread about and destroyed in that Village, and the rest of the Parish, though a small one, between two and three hundred Persons. But notwithstanding this so great Violence of the Disease, it was restrained from reaching beyond that Parish by the Care of the Rector; from whose Son, and another worthy Gentleman, I have the Relation. This Clergyman advised, that the Sick should be removed into Hutts or Barracks built upon the Common; and procuring by the Interest of the then Earl of Devonshire, that the People should be well furnished with Provisions, he took effectual Care, that no one should go out of the Parish: and by this means he protected his Neighbours from Infection with compleat Success."

From *A General Chronological History of the Air* - T. Short - Vol i - 1749 pp 339-340

"In December 1664, some Families near Westminster were seized with the Plague, which was lately imported from Holland in some Bales of Cotton. However the violence of the severe and long Frost put a Stop to it, till April that it began again; was in a fluctuating State all May and June; after that rose to its Height before the Middle of September; then declined, and was out by the next Winter. The Fault not being in the Air, it spread no further than it was communicated. As to Eyam in Derbyshire, whither it was transmitted in a Letter from London with some Patterns of Cloth and Fashions to a Taylor, here it quickly killed between 2 and 300, or near half the People of the Village."

APPENDIX II

The Sources Used in this Study

The principal source for the present study is the parish register.[20] Additional information has been obtained from Hearth Tax returns, from a petition and from a number of wills.

The Hearth Tax returns for 1662, 1664 and 1667 are in the Public Record Office.[21] In them the parish is divided into three areas, Eyam township (i.e. the village and the surrounding administrative area), Foolow and the surrounding areas and Eyam Woodlands, the north-east corner of the parish. The 1662 return lists the names of those occupying (or possibly in some cases, owning) the 'charged' houses only, and contains forty-eight names for Eyam township, forty-three for Foolow and twenty-six for Eyam Woodlands. The 1664 list contains names for both charged and uncharged houses and so is potentially more valuable, but unfortunately is damaged and not completely legible. It contains sixty names for charged houses in Eyam township. The list for uncharged houses contains about one hundred names, but this is the damaged part of the manuscript and only some eighty can be traced to Eyam. The remainder may refer to the adjacent village of Stoney Middleton. The list for Foolow contains only nineteen names and that for Woodlands is missing. The 1672 list may be a list of arrears only. It contains fifty-five names for Eyam township, thirty-three for Foolow and the Woodlands list again is missing.

The petition, which is in the Saville collection in the Nottinghamshire County Record Office, is undated but must be either 1661 or 1662. It desires Sir George Saville to continue the Reverend Thomas Stanley as Rector and contains sixty-six names, all but four being completely legible. This petition and the wills have been used to confirm the presence in the parish of the named persons at the given date.

The parish register is a copy, apparently made about 1705. It appears to be a careful copy, for comparison with the Bishops Transcripts does not reveal more discrepancies than one often - perhaps usually - finds even with original registers, apart from the register gaps mentioned below.

The register commences in August 1630. There are two gaps, from February 1644 (New Style) to January 1645 and from November 1662 to March 1663, the latter gap being covered by the Bishops Transcripts. Over most of the period under review baptisms and burials of children record the names of both father and mother. In the following periods, however, the name of the father only is usually given, reducing the value of the register for reconstitution purposes:

August 1630 to August 1644	March 1665 to August 1665
November 1663 to September 1664	March 1667 to November 1669

The Bishops Transcripts of the register (copies sent to the Registry of the Diocese of Lichfield at intervals of roughly three years) are in the Lichfield Record Office. They commence in 1660, and those for the period 1660 to 1668 were compared with the parish register with the following results:

Year	No. of entries in register	No. of entries in register but not in transcript	No. of entries in transcript but not in register	Serious discrepancies between register and transcript
1660	64	2	2	1
1661	68	0	4	1
1662			19*	3
1663			35*	1
1664	76	0	4	2
1665	107	3	4	4
1666	279	6	0	5
1667	74	0	0	0

*These refer to the gaps in the register mentioned above.

The Methods Used in the Analysis

The parish register has been subjected to two different kinds of analysis. In the aggregative analysis, attention is directed to the monthly or annual totals of the baptisms, marriages and burials recorded in the register and to the way in which these totals vary with the passage of time.

The annual totals for these vital events are given in columns 1, 3 and 5.of Table 1. Since the vital events in a given year are subject to a number of chance influences, the annual totals are subject to irregular fluctuations and the underlying trends in them are difficult to detect. The annual totals have, therefore, been smoothed by taking five-year moving averages, and these are given in columns 2, 4 and 6 of the same Table.

The Natural Increase for each year, that is the excess of baptisms over burials (which may, of course, be negative), is given in column 7. The Cumulative Natural Increase is obtained by successively adding the annual natural increases and is given in column 8.and graphed in Figure 2. It will be seen, for example, that the total excess of baptisms over burials from the end of 1630 to the end of 1660 is 183.

In order to exhibit the course of the plague, the number of burials for each week of the period March 1665 to December 1666 has been calculated and these weekly totals are graphed in Figure 3.

In all these Tables, register entries clearly relating to persons resident outside the parish have been disregarded and entries in the Bishops Transcripts additional to those in the register have been added.

Reconstitution and the tables derived from it.

Reconstitution is an attempt to use the information given in the parish register to reconstruct as many families as possible. A marriage is recorded on a form reproduced in Figure 1, and the baptisms and burials associated with that marriage are added. In some cases, though the marriage is not recorded (it may, for example, have taken place in a neighbouring parish), the baptisms and burials of children indicate the existence of a family and are recorded in the same way.

There are a number of difficulties in reconstitution. The omission of a baptism or a burial from the register, either through error or because it took place in another parish, obviously causes a gap in the reconstitution. And if there are, at the same time, two heads of family with the same Christian name and surname, difficulty may arise in assigning a child to one or the other in the periods when the register did not also give the Christian name of the mother. Another difficulty arises with elderly people and with unmarried adults. They may well be represented in the register only by a record of their burial, and it is often impossible to assign them to a family even though, especially in the case of an elderly widow or widower, they may have been living in one. Lodgers, too, cannot be placed in the household with which they lived. In some cases a family can be reconstituted with virtual certainty. In others, the reconstitution may have a very high degree of probability. Nothing less than this is admitted.

One unexpected difficulty arose. There were a number of cases, especially in the two decades 1641-1660, where the reconstitution had all the appearance of a man remarrying, except that there was no record of the burial of the first wife. There were, it seemed to me, too many such cases for it to be due to under-registration, that is from the omission of a burial entry from the register. Another possibility was that these wives originated in a neighbouring parish and were buried there, but the printed register of Hathersage, with which Eyam had close connections, produced no burials of any of the missing wives, though it did produce marriages, baptisms and burials for other persons stated as being 'of Eyam'. A third possibility is that there may have been a considerable degree of common-law marriage in this period. This possibility is supported by the fact that the aggregation showed very high ratios of baptisms to marriages at this time, suggesting unrecorded unions, and further support comes from an article by Dr. E.A. Wrigley on Clandestine Marriage in *Local Population Studies*[22]

In spite of these difficulties, a very considerable number of families were reconstituted and it has been possible to examine the course of the plague epidemic in families affected by it and to derive useful statistics. Tables II to IX have been derived from the reconstitution.

Notes

1. *A History of Epidemics in Britain* - Charles Creighton - Cambridge University Press 1894. Second edition, Frank Cass and Co, 1965.
2. See pp 11-23 'Some Medical Aspects of Plague'.
3. 'The Plague of Eyam: A Tercentenary Re-evaluation' - G.R. Batho - in the *Journal of the Derbyshire Archaeological and Natural History Society LXXXIV 1964*.
4. *The Conquest of Plague* - L.F. Hirst - Oxford University Press, 1953.
5. *A History of Bubonic Plague in the British Isles* - J.F.D. Shrewsbury - Cambridge University Press, 1970.
6. Confirmed in a communication from Professor J.N. Tarn, Roscoe Professor of Architecture in the University of Liverpool.
7. *The History of Derby from the remote ages of antiquity to the year MDCCXCI* W. Hutton, 1791.
8. *Plague* - R. Pollitzer - World Health Organisation, Geneva, 1954. p 485.
9. *A Treatise on Pneumonic Plague* - Wu Lien Teh - World Health Organisation, Geneva, 1926. p. 522.
10. *The Great Plague in London in 1665* - W.G. Bell - London 1924. 2nd edn.
11. Shrewsbury pp 104, 124-5, 159, 224, 333, 402, 475.
12. *A General Chronological History of the Air* - T. Short, 1749, pp 339-343.
13. Article in *Brit. Encyc. Med. Pract.* IX p. 676.
14. Pollitzer p. 504.
15. 'Plague Mortality by Age and Sex in the Parish of St. Botolph's without Bishopgate, London 1603' - M.F. and T.H. Hollingsworth - in *Population Studies* XXV 1971.
16. 'Crisis Mortality' - R.S. Schofield - in *Local Population Studies* No.9, Autumn 1972.
17. Appendix 1.
18. Shrewsbury p. 181. His argument is that the rat fleas brought into the house by the first victim would desert their human host for their preferred rat host and infect it with plague. On its death, its fleas, now also infected, could attack humans and cause plague in them. He calculated that the whole process would take about fourteen days.
19. Mompesson's policy, however courageous and well intentioned, was based on erroneous views of the causation and transmission of plague, and modern authorities are agreed that it was mistaken. It is interesting to note that as early as 1744, when there were fears of the re-importation of plague into England, the physician, Richard Mead attacked the policy of segregation in his *Discourse on the Plague,* writing 'For confining people and shutting them up together in great numbers will make the distemper rage with augmented force..... For these reasons, I think, to allow people with proper cautions to remove from an infected place is the best means to suppress the contagion'.
20. I am indebted to the Rector of Eyam, the Revd. E.M. Turner, for permission to use the register.
21. P.R.O. E179/94/378, E179/94/403, E179/245/7, E179/245/9 pt. 2.
22. 'Clandestine Marriages in Tetbury in the late 17th Century' E.A. Wrigley - in *Local Population Studies* No. 10, Spring 1973.

Figure I

MARRIAGE

no.	place	date	date of end	date of next
M / 1.2 /	EYAM	/ 2.2.1664 /	||	

LITERACY

husband	wife
L /	/

HUSBAND

surname	name(s)	date of baptism(birth)	date of burial (death)	order of marr.	earlier FRF no.	later FRF no.	residence at baptism
H / BOCKIN /	RICHARD /	14.10.1638 /	26.11.1693 /	1 /	/	/	/

residence (occupation) at marriage	residence (occupation) at burial	date	residence (occupation)	date	residence (occupation)
/	/	/	/	/	/

Husband's father

surname	name(s)	residence (occupation)	FRF no.
HF /	THOMAS /	/	/

Husband's mother

surname	name(s)
HM /	ANNE /

WIFE

surname	name(s)	date of baptism(birth)	date of burial (death)	order of marr.	earlier FRF no.	later FRF no.	residence at baptism
W / BENNETT /	ELLEN /	/	/	/	/	/	/

residence (occupation) at marriage	residence (occupation) at burial	date	residence (occupation)	date	residence (occupation)
/	/	/	/	/	/

Wife's father

surname	name(s)	residence (occupation)	FRF no.
WF /	/	/	/

Wife's mother

surname	name(s)
WM /	/

CHILDREN

	sex	date of baptism(birth)	date of burial (death)	status	name(s)	date of marriage	FRF no. of first marr	surname of spouse	age at bur.	age at marr.	birth inter-val	age of mother
1	C /F/	23.11.1664	/ /	/	ANNE	/	/					
2	C /M/	6.2.1670	20.5.1673	/	FRANCIS	/	/					
3	C /F/		22.9.1671	/	EMM	/	/					
4	C /F/		23.10.1674	/	BRIGITT	/	/					
5	C /F/	6.12.1675	15.8.1688	/	ELLEN	/	/					
6	C /F/	30.6.1677	25.6.1700	/	ALICE	/	/					
7	C /F/	24.10.1680	/	/	SARAH	/	/					
8	C / /	/	/ /	/		/	/					
9	C / /	/	/ /	/		/	/					
10	C / /	/	/ /	/		/	/					
11	C / /	/	/ /	/		/	/					
12	C / /	/	/ /	/		/	/					
13	C / /	/	/ /	/		/	/					
14	C / /	/	/ /	/		/	/					
15	C / /	/	/ /	/		/	/					
16	C / /	/	/ /	/		/	/					

COMMENTS		Husband	Wife	Age group	Years marr.	No of births
LIT 1664 UNCHANGED.	Age at marriage			15 - 19		
	Age at end of marriage			20 - 24		
* Mentioned in will of Anne Bennett, vicar, 1689.	Age at burial			25 - 29		
	Length of widowhood (mths)			30 - 34		
	Length of marriage (years)			35 - 39		
	Number of births	total	sons	daughters	40 - 44	
FRF iv 67				45 - 49		

Figure 2. Cumulative Natural Increases

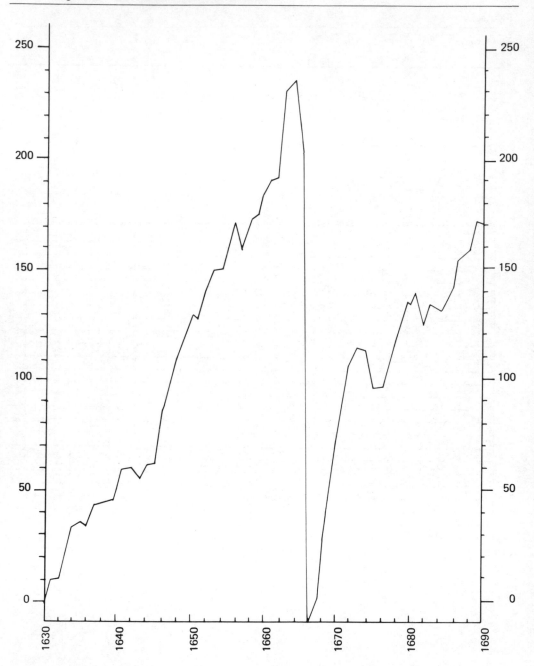

Figure 3   Weekly Totals of Burials

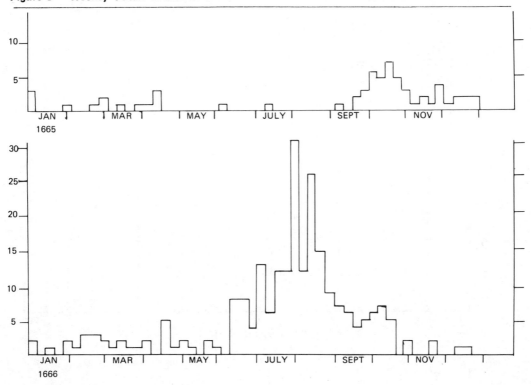

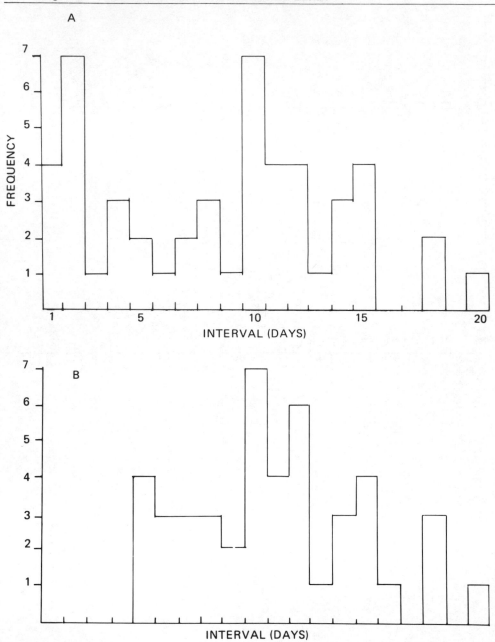

Figure 4.   Interval Between First and Second Burials

88

Table I Aggregative Data from the Parish Register

Year	Baptisms (1)	(2)	Burials (3)	(4)	Marriages (5)	(6)	(7)	(8)
1631	22		11		1		11	11
2	29		29		9		0	11
3	30	30	25	22	9	5.0	5	16
4	32	31	15	26	4	6.8	17	33
5	35	30	31	23	2	5.8	4	37
6	31	29	32	23	10	4.6	−1	36
7	21	29	14	26	4	5.4	7	43
8	26	29	24	26	3	5.6	2	45
9	32	29	31	24	8	4.2	1	46
1640	34	32	29	28	3	4.2	5	51
	292		**241**		**53**			
1641	30	29	21	27*	3	4.0	9	60
2	37	28*	36	25*	4	3.2*	1	61
3	13	27*	19*	25*	2	4.0*	−6*	55
4	27*	29*	21*	25*	4*	5.6*	6*	61
5	30*	28*	28*	20*	7*	5.2*	2*	63
6	39	30*	19	19*	11	4.8*	20	83
7	30	31*	14	19*	2	4.4	16	99
8	25	30	14	17	0	3.8	11	110
9	29	28	21	19	2	2.2	8	118
1650	28	28	16	20	4	2.6	12	130
	288		**209**		**39**			
1651	28	29	29	21	3	4.4	−1	129
2	32	29	19	22	4	4.0	13	142
3	27	31	21	24	9	3.2	6	148
4	30	31	27	22	0	2.6	3	151
5	38	30	26	26	0	2.6	12	163
6	28	31	19	27	0	1.4	9	172
7	27	31	39	27	4	2.2	−12	160
8	33	30	22	27	3	3.8	11	171
9	31	32	28	29	4	4.6	3	174
1660	32	33	23	27	8	6.6	9	183
	306		**253**		**35**			

continued

	Baptisms		Burials		Marriages			
1661	36	36	30	27	4	8.2	6	189
2	35	38	32	26	14	10.0	3	192
3	48	(38)	19	(34)	11	(10.8)	29	221
4	41	(34)	26	(74)	13	(10.4)	15	236
5	31	(34)	62	(73)	12	(10.2)	−31	205
6	16	(35)	232	(73)	2	(11.4)	−216	−11
7	34	(35)	25	(74)	13	(11.0)	9	−2
8	53	(39)	22	(66)	17	(9.4)	31	29
9	42	44	28	23	11	10.8	14	43
1670	50	44	21	22	4	9.0	29	72
	386		497		101			
1671	42	39	20	21	9	6.1	22	94
2	35	34	20	20	4	5.0	15	109
3	26	29	18	24	3	4.8	8	117
4	19	26	23	25	5	4.6	−4	113
5	23	26	41	26	3	5.6	−18	95
6	26	27	25	27	8	5.6	1	96
7	35	30	25	27	9	6.0	10	106
8	31	32	19	24	3	6.2	12	118
9	34	33	25	24	7	5.6	9	127
1680	34	30	27	26	4	4.8	7	134
	305		243		55			
1681	30	30	25	27	5	5.4	5	139
2	22	28	36	27	5	4.2	−14	125
3	31	25	20	25	6	4.2	11	136
4	24	25	28	24	1	3.6	−4	132
5	20	26	14	21	4	3.8	6	138
6	27	26	23	22	2	4.2	4	142
7	30	27	18	19	6	5.0	12	154
8	31	28	26	22	8	5.2	5	159
9	28		16		5		12	171
1690	25		26		5		−1	170
	268		232		47			

Columns 1, 3 and 5 are annual totals from the register.
Columns 2, 4 and 6 are five-year moving averages of these totals.
Column 7 is the annual natural increase.
Column 8 is the cumulative natural increase.

Asterisks denote that the register was faulty so that the figures given are estimates or moving averages derived from them.
Moving averages in brackets involve the totals for the exceptional plague years.

Table II Familes with Recorded Burials in the Plague Period

	Total		Outlying		Eyam township		Unknown	
					Situation			
1. Families in which all members died.		17	1	(1)	10	(32)	6	(24)
2. Families in which both husband and wife survived, with or without children.								
a. later baptisms recorded	4	8	1	(1)	4	(5)	3	(6)
b. no later baptisms recorded	4							
3. Families in which husband survived (sometimes already widower) with or without children.								
a. remarried after plague period	8	15	3	(6)	7	(19)	5	(10)
b. no remarriage, but later evidence of existence of members of family	4							
c. no further record in register.	3							
4. Families in which wife survived (sometimes already widow) with or without children.								
a. remarried after plague period	5	29	1	(1)	20	(48)	8	(17)
b. no remarriage but later evidence of existence of members of family	10							
c. no further record in register.	14							
5. Families in which children only survived.								
a. later evidence of existence of members of family	5	20	5	(34)	13	(42)	2	(7)
b. no further record in register	15							
		89	11	(43)	54	(146)	24	(64)
BURIALS OF SINGLE PERSONS WHO COULD NOT BE ASCRIBED TO A FAMILY		16	1	(1)	2	(2)	13	(13)
BURIALS DISREGARDED IN ABOVE ANALYSIS (SEE PAGE)				(4)		(2)		(1)
TOTAL BURIALS				(48)		(150)		(78)

(Figures in brackets are the actual numbers of burials associated with each group.)

91

Table III — Number Of Burials Per Family In Plague Period

Number of burials per family	1	2	3	4	5	6	7	8	9	10	11	
Number of such families	25	22	20	10	4	3	3	0	1	0	1	(89)

Table IV — Families without burials in the plague period, but known to be in being in the five years preceding the plague. (See page 74)

	Total	Situation		
		Outlying	Eyam township	Unknown
1. Families with recorded marriages or baptisms after the plague	62	28	16	18
2. Families with burials, marriages of children, or Hearth Tax recorded after plague, but no baptisms.	74	33	27	14
3. Families which had no record in register or Hearth Tax after plague.	21	9	7	5
	157	70	50	37

Table V — Persistence of families during plague

1.	Known or likely to have persisted	172
2.	No evidence of persistence, but not known to have become extinct.	57
3.	Became extinct	17
		246

Table VI — New families recorded between the end of October 1666 and the end of December 1676.

	1666	67	68	69	70	71	72	73	74	75	76	Total
1. Head probably related to a pre-plague family) a. son		7	3	6	1	2	1	3	0	1	1	25
) b. relationship not determined	1	4	11	2	5	3	1	0	2	1	2	32
	1	11	14	8	6	5	2	3	2	2	3	57
2. No apparent relationship with pre-plague family		3	1	1	3	1	1	2	1	0	0	13

Table VII   Analysis of all baptisms 1667-1670

	To pre-plague families		To post-plague families		Unknown	Outlying	Situation Eyam township	Unknown	Total
	No	%	No	%	No				
1667	27	79	7	21	0	14	10	10	34
1668	35	66	16	30	2	13	15	25	53
1669	23	55	19	45	0	12	9	21	42
1670	16	32	33	66	1	11	7	32	50
	101		75		3	50	41	88	179

Table VIII   Age at burial

Period		0 to 1 month		1 month to 1 year		1 + years to 5 years		5 + years to 10 years		10+ years to 20 years		Over 20 years		Unknown		Total
		No	%	No	%	No	%	No	%	No	%	No	%	No	%	
1651	M	16	11.3	16	11.3	16	11.3	5	3.5	7	5.0	62	44.0	19	13.5	141
to	F	5	4.3	15	12.9	16	13.8	1	0.9	7	6.0	56	48.3	16	13.8	116
1660	T	21	8.1	31	12.1	32	12.5	6	2.3	14	5.4	118	45.9	35	13.6	257
Annual average		2.1		3.1		3.2		0.6		1.4		11.8		3.5		25.7
1661	M	6	10.9*	4	7.2	9	16.4	3	5.5	2	3.6	27	49.1	4	7.2	55
to	F	7	14.9*	3	6.4	5	10.6	1	2.1	3	6.4	26	55.3	2	4.3	47
1664	T	13	12.7	7	6.9	14	13.7	4	3.9	5	4.9	53	51.9	6	5.9	102
Annual average		3.3		1.8		3.5		1.0		1.3		13.3		1.5		25.5
14	M	6	4.2*	2	1.4	11	7.6	15	10.4	24	16.7	67	46.5	19	13.2	144
plague	F	2	1.5*	6	4.5	10	7.6	10	7.6	25	18.9	66	50.0	13	9.8	132
months	T	8	2.9	8	2.9	21	7.6	25	9.1	49	17.8	133	48.2	32	11.6	276
Annual average	+	6.9		6.9		18.0		21.4		42.0		114.0		27.4		236.6
1667	M	3	6.1	3	6.1	2	4.1	0	0.0	2	4.1	29	59.2	10	20.4	49
to	F	7	14.9	5	10.6	3	6.4	2	4.3	1	2.1	22	46.8	7	14.9	47
1670	T	10	10.4	8	8.3	5	5.2	2	2.1	3	3.1	51	53.1	17	17.7	96
Annual average		2.5		2.0		1.3		0.5		0.8		12.8		4.3		24.0
1671	M	12	11.0	8	7.3	7	6.4	5	4.6	1	0.9	60	55.0	16	14.7	109
to	F	8	6.2	6	4.6	6	4.6	2	1.5	7	5.4	87	66.9	14	10.8	130
1680	T	20	8.4	14	5.9	13	5.4	7	2.9	8	3.3	147	61.5	30	12.6	239
Annual average		2.0		1.4		1.3		0.7		0.8		14.7		3.0		23.9

M — Male   F — Female   T — Total

* Possible difficulties over distribution of infant burials between M and F.
+ i.e., reduced by a ratio of 12/14.

Table IX   Time-interval between first and second burial.

Interval (days)	Frequency A	B
1	4*	
2	7*	
3	1*	
4	3*	
5	2	4
6	1	3
7	2	3
8	3	3
9	1	2
10	7	7
11	4	4
12	4	6
13	1	1
14	3	3
15	4	4
16	0	1
17	0	0
18	2	3
19	0	0
20	1	1
21	2	2
22	0	0
23	0	0
24	1	1
25	0	0
26	2	2
27	0	0
28	0	0
29	0	0
30	0	0
31	1	re-allocated to 10
35	1	re-allocated to 21
40	1	1
62	1	1
90	1	1

In column B the cases asterisked in Column A have been re-allocated according to their second interval.

An Anatomy of an Epidemic:

Colyton, November 1645 to November 1646

Roger Schofield

When Tony Wrigley chose Colyton for his pioneering application of the technique of family reconstitution to English parish registers, he made this market town in south-east Devon instantly famous in the community of historical demographers and local population historians.[1] The three features of Colyton's varied demographic history that most people remember all occurred in the seventeenth century: the high age at which women married towards the end of the century, the evidence for deliberate control of fertility at about the same time, and the great mortality crisis of 1645-6, which dominates the graph of the vital events recorded in the parish register (Figure 1).

Figure 1   Baptisms, burials and marriages in Colyton (nine-year moving averages)

Source: Colyton parish register.

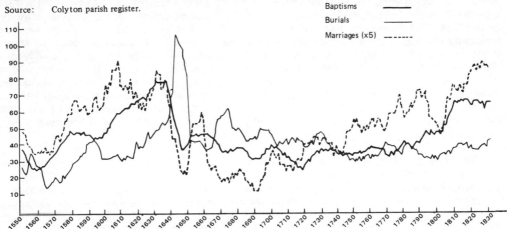

95

These dramatic changes in nuptiality and fertility have been extensively discussed, but very little has been written about the crisis of 1645-6.[2] Yet it is of considerable interest and importance, if only because of its catastrophic impact on the population. In his original article Tony Wrigley estimated that about one-fifth of the inhabitants of Colyton died during the epidemic, which he identified as 'in all probability... a last and virulent outbreak of bubonic plague.'[3] Since the Colyton register is silent as to the cause of death it might be instructive to test the plausibility of this identification by investigating the epidemic in somewhat greater detail, and comparing it with two well-researched epidemics of bubonic plague: St Botolph's without Bishopsgate (London) in 1603, and Eyam (Derbyshire) in 1665-6.[4]

I shall begin by considering how far some of the more obvious characteristics of an historical epidemic, for example its length, severity, seasonal incidence and geographical spread, can provide clues as to the disease underlying it. I shall then examine the impact of epidemic mortality in greater detail, paying particular attention to the degree to which it was selective in its incidence on certain families or age-groups. Finally I shall consider the consequences of the epidemic for the demography and economy of Colyton.

The parish of Colyton comprised a main settlement, and a number of outlying hamlets and farms.[5] The main settlement, Colyton Town, was situated on the River Coly near where it joins the river Axe, about three miles from the south coast. The largest hamlet in the parish was Colyford which lay astride the main road running from Exeter to Lyme Regis, about a mile south of the town. The parish was therefore open to contact with travellers and the wider world, especially in the early seventeenth century when this part of Devon was heavily engaged in the manufacture of woollen cloth.[6] This is a point of some importance because Paul Slack has found that in the sixteenth and early seventeenth centuries bubonic plague in Devon was largely confined to the market towns and large villages situated near the coast and easily accessible to the outside world.[7] Furthermore, in the mid-1640s military activities increased the amount of movement in this part of the country, and the Colyton register records the burial of twenty soldiers between January 1644 and September 1645. Indeed in October 1645, about a month before the epidemic began, a strong force of Royalist troops was stationed at Ottery St Mary, about ten miles west of Colyton.[8] On 13th October General Fairfax, recently victorious at the siege of Bristol, sent a small detachment of the New Model Army to Axminster (five miles from Colyton), the main body of the army remaining encamped at Chard, some ten miles to the north-east.[9] The next day the New Model Army marched from Chard, through Axminster to Honiton, probably along a road which took them within three miles of Colyton Town. The Royalists then withdrew to the other side of Exeter, and Fairfax went on to Collumpton, Tiverton and Crediton.[10] However, about two weeks later, on 4th November, the parliamentary army doubled back and took up quarters in Ottery St Mary, which had been vacated by the Royalists. But they soon found themselves caught up in a rapidly escalating epidemic, and after five weeks, on December 6th, they moved on again to Tiverton.[11]

There was therefore considerable military movement in the immediate vicinity of Colyton in the month before the epidemic broke out, but it is difficult to establish any link between the two occurrences. The main army itself never visited Colyton, though small detachments of troops may have done so. Furthermore, the parliamentary forces were not always carriers of disease. They somehow managed to avoid contracting the plague that was raging inside Bristol when they captured it,[12] and although they suffered in Ottery St Mary, they carried nothing with them to Tiverton, even though the Royalists had suffered tremendous mortality there the year before.[13] The lack of any epidemic in Tiverton suggests that Ottery may have infected the army, rather than vice-versa.

Unfortunately the Ottery epidemic remains shrouded in mystery because the register, after recording a massive increase in the number of burials in December 1645 and January 1646 then breaks off until May 1648. Fairfax's chaplain, Joshua Sprigge, writes rather cryptically of the Ottery epidemic that

'Colonel Pickering, and divers other officers, died of the new disease in that place; six of the general's own family were sick of it at one time, and throughout the foot regiment half the soldiers.'[14]

The high proportion infected, and the implication of a low proportion dying, suggest a highly infectious disease with only a moderate case fatality rate. Interestingly Sprigge mentioned neither typhus nor plague, though both he and the army were familiar with them.

But just as we are unable to establish any connection between the army and Colyton, so the link between the epidemics at Ottery and Colyton eludes us. We would have some grounds for alleging such a link if we could find signs of epidemic mortality in other parishes in the area around these two parishes. But one of the most striking features of the Colyton epidemic is its isolation. On the broader, regional, canvas there is some scattered evidence of plague in Devon in July and September 1646, when the Colyton epidemic had been raging for several months, and again in January and April 1647, when it was all over.[15] On a more local level, a search of the registers of thirteen parishes not more than fifteen miles from Colyton reveals that in ten cases there was no rise in the number of burials recorded during the period of the Colyton epidemic.[16] The three exceptions are all market towns, although other market towns experienced no rise. Ottery St Mary we have already discussed; the other two were Pitminster, where burials were running at about three times their normal level in 1645, but not in 1646; and Hemyock, where burials were very high for a short period between June and August 1646. Even more remarkably, none of the seven parishes immediately adjacent to Colyton showed any sign of a significant increase in the number of burials recorded while the Colyton epidemic was raging.[17]

The lack of any other evidence of 'crisis' mortality either in south-east Devon or in the immediate vicinity of Colyton points to the epidemics in Colyton and Ottery being isolated occurrences. If there was a link between them it must have been a direct one, by-passing the neighbouring communities. Furthermore the absence of any generally high mortality in the region would seem to rule out more general explanations such as climatic conditions or harvest failure. The latter, in any case, is scarcely a serious contender since the Exeter price series indicates that the harvest of 1645 was normal, and although the harvest of 1646 was deficient, the Colyton epidemic was almost over by then.[18] According to Short, writing in the eighteenth century, '1645 and Part of 1646, [were] extremely hot and dry.'[19]

More significantly the fact that the epidemic failed to spread from Colyton to the neighbouring communities makes it unlikely that the disease behind the 'crisis' mortality was spread by airborne infection. As we have already noticed, Colyton was a market town in a pastoral area, involved in textile manufacture, and therefore presumably much visited by the inhabitants of the surrounding villages. Whatever the disease may have been, it was apparently not one to be contracted in a public place, for example at a market, and carried back to infect other communities. On the other hand, when mortality largely due to airborne infection did strike the region, as seems to have been the case in the years 1727-32,[20] it was both more widespread and more modest in its severity. A study of twelve Exeter parishes and twenty-eight parishes within a radius of about ten miles of the city shows that the numbers of burials rose to over one and a half times their normal level in 75% of the city parishes and 57% of the country parishes.[21]

The isolation of the Colyton epidemic makes it difficult to associate the mortality with a disease spread by airborne infection, and as a glance at the rough checklist of the characteristics of common epidemic diseases contained in Appendix 1 will show, this would tend to suggest that the epidemic was not caused by diseases such as diphtheria, influenza and small-pox. Diseases such as dysentery, typhoid, plague and typhus, which are spread in other ways, would seem to be more consistent with the restricted geographical spread of the Colyton epidemic.

The inference we have drawn from the geographical aspect of the epidemic, although powerful, is rather negative in character. Can we learn anything more positive by studying the severity and timing of the 'crisis' mortality? The Colyton epidemic was undoubtedly severe: we have already seen that the death rate was estimated at about 20%. Since the normal death rate was about 3% per annum, and the Colyton epidemic lasted slightly over a year, an epidemic death rate of 20% implies almost a sevenfold increase in the number of burials being recorded. This is confirmed by the numbers of burials recorded in the parish register. In Colyton the 'annual' frequency in the ten years before the epidemic was 67.4 burials, but this period includes three years (1643, 1644 and 1645) in which considerably more burials were recorded than usual. If a slightly earlier pre-crisis period is taken, from 1633 to 1642, the 'annual' frequency is a little lower at 52.4. The 'annual' frequency recorded during the epidemic was 371.1, giving an increase over the immediate pre-crisis period of 5.5 times, and an increase over the slightly earlier period of 7.1 times.

A death rate of 20%, or a sevenfold increase in the number of burials recorded, constitutes an exceptionally severe epidemic. Most epidemics recorded in the parish registers involved only two or threefold increases in the normal level of burials, and a fourfold increase was unusually high. Increases of more than sixfold are rare outside the inner parishes of large cities, indeed amongst a collection of some 404 aggregative analyses of registers, there are only nine non-urban parishes with epidemics of this scale, of which Colyton is one.[22] All except two are market towns of roughly the same size as Colyton, and in every case there is either direct evidence, or a very strong presumption, that the epidemic was due to plague.[23]

Indeed to attain a death rate of this magnitude requires either a disease with a very high case fatality rate, such as bubonic plague, or a disease with a lower case fatality rate which is so infectious that a very substantial proportion of the population is affected. Although the case fatality rates given in Appendix 1 are necessarily very approximate, it is clear that some diseases have such low death rates that they are unlikely to be able to produce an overall death rate of 20% even if everyone in the population were infected. Dysentery, diphtheria, smallpox and typhus occasionally produce high enough case fatality rates to produce an overall death rate of 20%, but an unusually high proportion of the population would have to be infected.[24] Influenza is more problematical; although highly infectious it is not very lethal: for example the case fatality rate in India during the unusually virulent 1918 pandemic was between 10% and 13%.[25] Whether earlier, historical, outbreaks of influenza were more lethal must remain an open question.

In this connection it is perhaps worth noting that mortality in the two comparative outbreaks of bubonic plague in the seventeenth century was also very high. During the six months of plague in St Botolph's without Bishopsgate, London, in 1603, the 'annual' burial frequency shot up from a pre-crisis level of 147.6 to a phenomenal 2844, an increase of 19.3 times.[26] We have already remarked that increases in epidemic mortality were much higher in urban parishes, and the increase recorded in our second example is more modest. The 'annual' number of burials in Eyam, Derbyshire in 1665-6 rose from a pre-crisis frequency of 25.6 (1651-64) to 239.9 during the plague epidemic, giving an increase of 9.4 times, much nearer to the 5.5 to 7.1 increase recorded in Colyton.[27]

The severity of the 'crisis' mortality in Colyton therefore suggests two alternative scenarios: a localised outbreak of a relatively lethal disease such as bubonic plague, or a considerably more widespread infection by one of a number of less deadly diseases. If we are right in concluding from the failure of the epidemic to spread to neighbouring communities that it was probably not an airborne infection that was at work, the alternative to bubonic plague is effectively narrowed down to dysentery or typhus. Does the timing of the epidemic help us to determine between these possibilities.

Although silent as to the cause of the epidemic, the Colyton register is at least explicit as to when it began and when it ended. In the margin beside a burial entry for 18 November 1645 a contemporary hand notes: 'when the sikness began'. And just over thirteen months later, beside an entry on 26 November 1646, the same hand notes: 'here the siknes ended'. These marginal notes appear to have been written by John Wilkins who was presented to the living of Colyton on 19 September 1647, and ejected in 1662.[28] The identification of the beginning and end of 'the siknes' was therefore probably made at least one year after the event, and it is not known whether Wilkins was resident in Colyton during the epidemic or whether he relied on the evidence of others. At all events 'the siknes' by no means followed an even course during these thirteen months.

Figure 2   Weekly burial frequencies in Colyton from 18 November 1645 to 27 November 1646.

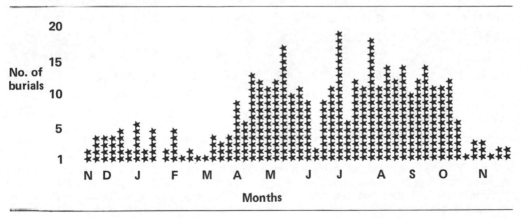

Source: Colyton parish register.

The course the epidemic took, week by week, is plotted in Figure 2. It began with between two and five burials being recorded each week, compared with 1.1 burials a week in the pre-crisis period. This new level continued until April 1646, when there was a rapid change of scale and the number of burials rose to between ten and fourteen a week, a level which persisted until the middle of October 1646. At one point, in mid-June, it looked as if the epidemic might peter out, but it returned with a vengeance and very high numbers of burials were recorded in early July. After mid-October the number of burials fell back to between two and five a week, and by the end of November the epidemic was over.

The monthly profile of the full thirteen months of the Colyton mortality is difficult to reconcile with the seasonal characteristics of any known disease. For example the large numbers of burials in the winter of 1645-6 favour a disease such as typhus or influenza.[29] But deaths from these diseases usually tail off during the summer, which is just when the number of burials in Colyton rises sharply. Both this rise, and the subsequent seasonal distribution of the burials, are much more consistent with either dysentery or bubonic plague.[30]

Not only does the Colyton epidemic span two different seasons, it also comprises two phases of rather different levels of mortality, corresponding to those seasons. Could it in fact be caused by two diseases rather than a single 'siknes'? There are two features of the epidemic mortality which might support this possibility. The first is that while the higher mortality of the summer and autumn of 1646 was accompanied by a substantial number of deaths occurring in quick succession in the same family, this feature was almost entirely absent in the lower mortality of the winter months.[31] Secondly, as is clear from Table 1, the numbers of burials recorded in these winter months were not much higher than those recorded in winters of the previous two years. Thus the winter mortality of 1645-6 may have been simply a slightly more severe visitation of an epidemic disease that had struck more than once before.

Table 1   Monthly burial frequencies in Colyton

Year	Jan	Feb	Mar	Apr	May	June	July	Aug	Sept	Oct	Nov	Dec
1633-42 (average)	4.4	5.2	5.2	4.8	4.4	3.9	4.2	3.4	3.4	4.8	3.8	4.9
1643	4	6	9	8	15	13	11	14	4	6	8	7
1644	12	2	15	5	8	11	10	5	9	6	12	7
1645	13	4	6	6	6	8	3	5	9	6	12	17
1646	15	9	12	42	56	35	56	60	49	32	8	2
1647	2	0	1	2	1	3	2	4	2	5	3	1

Source: Colyton parish register

Against the two-disease hypothesis is the explicit reference to a single 'siknes' in the parish register, although this description may not have been based on first-hand experience of the epidemic. Secondly, for bubonic plague, though not so easily for other diseases, it is possible to argue a case for a long epidemic with a monthly profile of the shape observed at Colyton. An altogether hypothetical sequence of events might run as follows. Bubonic plague is introduced into the community late in the year and fails to develop into a full-scale human epidemic because the low temperatures associated with late autumn and winter restrict the activity of the rat fleas.[32] There would be some plague mortality amongst the rat population, and occasionally the rat fleas, lacking their preferred hosts, would be active enough to seek out and infect a human. The warmer and wetter the winter months the more active and longer lived the rat fleas would be. When the temperature, and possibly the humidity, increased in the late spring or early summer, the rat fleas would live longer and become more active. As the mortality increased amongst the rat population, more rat fleas would successfully seek out humans and infect them with plague. Although burials would be higher than normal during the winter months, they would be sporadic compared to the increasing numbers produced in the warmer months, when climatic conditions finally allowed the disease to run through its normal epidemic cycle.

Interestingly enough the Colyton monthly profile of burials was paralleled by the pattern of events at Eyam, where plague first struck in September 1665 and epidemic mortality remained modest until the following June. Leslie Bradley, in commenting on this aspect of the Eyam epidemic, leaves open the question of whether the autumn infection persisted over the winter months to re-emerge in the summer of 1666. But the same pattern can also be observed both in some London parishes in the seventeenth century and in some Swedish parishes in the 1710-11 epidemic, where onsets of plague in the late autumn only developed into full scale epidemics in the following spring, and where the entries in the burial register explicitly identified plague as the cause of the increased mortality during the intervening winter months.[33]

Although there are only a few examples of plague persisting as a human epidemic through the inhospitable north European winter months, its persistence through the equally inhospitable hot and dry 'off season' in Asia is well attested. It is thought to survive there because the micro-climates of rodents' habitats continue to provide favourable conditions regardless of seasonal changes outside.[34] Since it is not inconceivable that a similar mechanism might operate in European conditions, particularly if the winter were warm and wet, the persistence of plague through an English winter must be entertained as a serious possibility.

Whatever the cause of the winter mortality at Colyton, and whatever the characteristics of winter plague may prove to be, the overwhelming proportion of epidemic deaths occurred during the summer months, and the long steep rise and fall of burials from April to November in 1646 looks like the classic profile of mortality from bubonic plague. Although none of the characteristics of the Colyton epidemic that we have considered so far are sufficiently conclusive to enable us to rule out some diseases altogether, the combination of a long and substantial summer peak in burials, a high overall death rate, and the lack of any epidemic mortality in neighbouring villages points strongly in the direction of bubonic plague. The most likely alternative explanation is a winter epidemic of typhus, coincidentally followed by a summer epidemic of dysentery or bubonic plague.

In order to narrow the field still further let us pursue the question of the geographical distribution of the epidemic mortality and examine its spread within the parish. Unfortunately the Colyton register ceased giving details of residence within the parish in 1611, so we shall have to adopt a different tactic and consider the pattern of deaths by family or household. But before we can do this we must consider how family patterns of mortality might be related to the different means by which diseases are transmitted.

Let us take as a first hypothesis the proposition that the more the chances of catching a disease depend on physical proximity to a localised source of infection, the more deaths will be clustered by household or family, so that some families will be affected whilst others, even near at hand, will escape. In the case of bubonic plague, for example, we would expect the chances of being bitten by an infected rat flea to be higher in a locality where rats had just died of plague than elsewhere. Since the black rat*(Rattus rattus)* generally stays close to human habitation, a person would be more likely to be infected by a flea in a house where rats had recently died, than by a rat flea hopping across either from a dead rat lying in the gutter, or from someone encountered in the street. Similarly, in the case of typhus, a person would be more likely to acquire an infected louse from someone who had just died in the room in which he was sleeping than from a casual encounter in the street. With airborne infections, on the other hand, transmission occurs much more readily as people breathe out infected droplets as they move around during their normal daily activities. Thus diseases like bubonic plague and typhus are likely to be associated with geographically clustered patterns of death, while airborne infections, such as influenza, will show much less clustering.

If we want to discover whether deaths were in fact clustered in families in a particular epidemic, we need to know what the distribution of deaths by family would have been if they had occurred randomly throughout the population. This is rather like the familiar problem of calculating how many times we should get different combinations of heads and tails if we were to spin different numbers of coins a large number of times. For example, if we were to spin a coin twice, there would be three possible combinations of heads and tails: both heads, one head and one tail, and both tails. With three spins there would be four combinations: all heads, two heads and one tail, one head and two tails, all tails. And so on for 'trials' of different numbers of spins. Fortunately there is a well-known formula, the 'binomial expansion', which enables us to calculate the number of times different combinations of heads and tails would occur in 'trials' of different numbers of spins.[35] If we substitute 'death' and 'survival' for 'heads' and 'tails', and 'family size' for a 'trial' of so many spins, we can use the binomial formula to calculate how many families of each size would have 0,1,2,3...etc. deaths The assumptions underlying this calculation are precisely those which underlie the coin-spinning analogy. Just as the chance of getting a 'head' must be constant from spin to spin, and independent of the result of any other spin in the 'trial', so the formula assumes that each individual's chance of dying is the same, and that it is independent of whether someone else, either in the family or elsewhere, happens to die or survive. In other words the binomial expansion gives us what we are seeking: the distribution of deaths by family we could expect if deaths in an epidemic occurred randomly throughout the population and independently of each other.

In order to calculate this distribution we need to know the chance of dying and the size of the family. This immediately raises the further question of whether the chance of dying in practice varied according to the size of the family. Historically there may have been several reasons for this. For example family size may have been associated with social or economic status, and families of different statuses may have had particular habits of diet or hygiene which made them more or less susceptible to certain diseases. Thus the clustering of deaths in families, and the variation in the death rate according to family size, are two logically separate aspects of epidemic mortality. They may both occur together, but they need not necessarily do so. I shall now argue that each is associated with a different aspect of the process by which epidemic disease is transmitted, and that the presence or absence of either of them may afford some indication of the general nature of the disease that underlies an epidemic.

Let us first consider a stylised picture of the transmission of a disease from an individual's point of view, confining our attention initially to diseases which are spread from person to person. At the risk of stating the obvious we can identify three distinct elements which determine whether an individual catches a disease or not:
(1) The chance of meeting someone with the disease outside the household.
(2) The chance of catching the disease from that person.
(3) Assuming that all members of a household meet each other, the chance of catching the disease from someone in the household.

To catch a disease outside the household a person must both meet someone carrying the disease and catch it from him. But everyone else in the household can do the same, and if we make the simplifying, although somewhat unreal, assumption that each member of the household is equally likely to catch the disease outside, then the number of members of the household catching the disease is directly related to the size of the household. We can use the binomial formula again to express our expectations under random conditions in more formal terms. If p is the chance of catching the disease and there are n people in a household, the average number of people infected in a series of 'trials' involving households of size n is np. If p is constant across households of all sizes then the number of people infected depends on the size of the household.

If the chance of catching the disease from other members of the household living in close physical proximity is high, we would expect that the numbers of infected people around, and hence the size of the household, would considerably influence an individual's chance of infection. Thus the size of household might be expected to be an important factor in catching diseases spread by contagion or by human parasites such as lice or fleas, for example typhus, or bubonic plague when the human flea is the significant vector. But if the members of the household were mobile and their chance of meeting an infected person outside the household and catching the disease from him were high, as might be the case during an epidemic of influenza or pneumonic plague, there would be little additional risk of infection from other members of the household, and we would expect only a weak association between the chance of infection and household size. Finally, if the chance of catching the disease from another member of the household is zero, then the number of infected people in the household is quite irrelevant, and an individual's chance of infection will have nothing to do with household size. Thus if bubonic plague is only introduced into households by rats and is only transmitted to man by the rat flea, never from man to man by the human flea, we would expect no association between the chance of infection and household size.

But households may differ systematically in various ways. The materials from which they are constructed may determine whether they are infested by animals carrying infected parasites, and their location may determine whether their inhabitants are likely to meet infected people in the world outside. For example, men and women living in isolated farmsteads may be less likely to meet infected people than would those living in a village street. Also the chance of catching a disease may be influenced by habits of diet, dress or hygiene, which may vary systematically with the social or economic status of the household. The more marked the differences between households, the more we would expect to find the incidence of disease clustered in certain households and absent in others.

The important point is that where systematic differences do obtain, they may refer to certain household characteristics, such as location or status, independently of their size. Thus the clustering of the incidence of disease in certain households may occur without any association of the incidence of the disease with household size. However, in practice it may be the case that a factor which produces systematic differences between households is also associated with household size. For example, households of framework knitters may be crammed together in thatched houses in a particular part of a village and they may be larger than the average size of household in the community. In such a case we might expect to find both a clustering of deaths by household and an association of the incidence of disease with household size.

Once we have made the logical distinction between the clustering of a disease in certain households and the association of its incidence with household size, we have a useful means of identifying the relative importance of different factors in the transmission of the disease. Thus we would expect the incidence of airborne infections, such as influenza or pneumonic plague, to be weakly clustered by household and strongly associated with household size. Diseases spread by contagion, for example dysentery, or by human parasite, for example typhus or bubonic plague through the human flea, might be expected to show a moderate clustering by household and a very strong association with household size. On the other hand, diseases spread by animal parasites, such as bubonic plague through the rat flea, would show marked differences between households, depending on the movement of the animal hosts, and this would be reflected in a strong clustering by household, quite independently of household size.

Thus, so far as bubonic plague is concerned, the distinction between household clustering and association with household size would also appear to provide a means of discriminating between the human flea and the rat flea as the significant vector in a given plague epidemic. Strong clustering by household would suggest the rat flea, while a strong association with household size would indicate the human flea. Unfortunately other factors may intervene to complicate the picture. For example, even if the human flea were the sole vector present, there might still be differences between households, say in their location, which might affect their members's chances of catching plague infected fleas, and be unconnected with household size. Conversely, even if the rat flea were the sole vector, an association between household size and some other factor, for example the density of rats, might produce an apparent association between the incidence of plague and the size of the household. Thus association with household size is not inconsistent with transmission of plague by the rat flea, nor is clustering by household incompatible with transmission by the human flea. Nevertheless our original statement still stands: a strong clustering of plague by household would indicate the rat flea, while a strong association with household size would point to the human flea as the significant vector. Unfortunately we can only rarely observe the actual incidence of disease in historical epidemics; the evidence we have usually relates to burials. But since we have no grounds to suspect that plague varied in its deadliness from household to household, it is probably fair to assume it to have been constant and to take the distribution of burials as a guide to the distribution of the disease.

In the case of Colyton there is a further, and severe, difficulty arising from the lack of a census of the parish at this date which we could use to identify the members of each household. But the family reconstitution forms (FRFs), which Tony Wrigley completed, contain the names of the members of nuclear families, that is husband and wife and their offspring.

Although nuclear families comprised the overwhelming majority of households in pre-industrial England, the nuclear families recorded on the FRFs by no means always corresponded to households.[36] For example, older children recorded on the FRFs may have left home to go into service, while elderly widows and widowers may have been living with other families or in institutions, rather than alone.

We can reduce the potential discrepancy between the residential household and the family as recorded on the FRF by considering only those FRFs where the whole family appears to be in observation during the epidemic, treating as absent any child who had married or reached the age of twenty by the time the epidemic began.[37] But even with these safeguards the population was probably more mixed residentially than appears from the FRFs. Thus our estimates of the effects of both clustering by household and household size on the distribution of burials in an epidemic are bound to be imperfect.

Table 2   Death rates by size of family, Colyton. Nov. 1645 - Nov. 1646

Size of family	Families	People	No. dying	% Dying* ± 95% confidence interval
1	39	39	8	21 ± 13
2	90	180	31	17 ± 6
3	86	258	32	12 ± 4
4	78	312	62	20 ± 4
5	38	190	47	25 ± 6
6	33	198	43	22 ± 6
7	21	147	32	22 ± 7
8+	21	189	43	23 ± 6
All	406	1513	298	20

*Percentages rounded to nearest whole number
Source: Family reconstitution forms as specified in note 25.

Unfortunately there were insufficient FRFs to allow meaningful calculations to be made for the winter months separately, so the following analysis relates to burials recorded during the whole epidemic.

The Colyton FRFs were sorted by size according to the number of people recorded on them who were still alive at the start of the epidemic. Table 2 shows the numbers of families of each size, the numbers of people at risk, and the numbers who died during the epidemic period.[39] The overall death rate was 20%, and the rate did not increase regularly with family size. Although the death rates of the larger families were generally slightly above the average, and those of some of the smaller sized families slightly below, the differences were not large. With the curious exception of the very low figure of 12% for families of three persons, the death rates all lie within 5% of the average, and there is a fair chance (more than one in twenty) that such small differences could be accounted for by the random variation associated with small samples.[40]

The lack of association between the size of family and the death rate may merely reflect a poor correspondence between the size of the families recorded on the FRFs and the size of the households in which members of the families were actually residing. It may also reflect the fact that some members of a household, for example very young children, were not so mobile as others, so that differences in the age composition of individual households may confuse the picture. But if physical proximity were an important factor in the transmission of the epidemic disease, one would expect to find considerable differences between the death rates of households as small as two and households as large as eight. The discrepancy between the residence patterns suggested by the FRFs and those that obtained in reality would have to be very great for a systematic variation of this magnitude to be eliminated. The balance of evidence would therefore seem to suggest that person-to-person transmission of the disease in close physical proximity was not an important element in the Colyton epidemic.

In order to investigate the second aspect of the incidence of an epidemic, namely how far burials were clustered in certain families and not in others, we need to have some idea of what the distribution of burials would have been like in the absence of any clustering by family. As we discovered above, if we assume that everyone's chance of dying was the same, and was independent of whether someone else in the same family had died or not, we can calculate for each size of family the number of families there would be with 0,1,2... etc. deaths.

Table 3   Observed and expected distributions of families, by size and number

Size of family	\multicolumn{12}{c}{Number dying in family}												All
	\multicolumn{2}{c}{0}	\multicolumn{2}{c}{1}	\multicolumn{2}{c}{2}	\multicolumn{2}{c}{3}	\multicolumn{2}{c}{4}	\multicolumn{2}{c}{5 & above*}	
	Obs.	Exp.	Obs.	Exp.	Obs.	Exp.	Obs.	Exp.	Obs.	Exp.	Obs.	Exp.	
1	31	31	8	8	.		.		.		.		39
2	63	61	23	25	4	3	.		.		.		90
3	65	58	12	25	7	3	2	0	.		.		86
4	45	32	15	32	10	12	5	2	3	0	.		78
5	15	9	13	15	2	10	3	3	4	1	1	0	38
6	17	8	5	13	2	9	3	3	5	1	1	0	33
7	8	4	4	7	3	6	3	3	2	1	1	0	21
8+	9	2	0	6	4	6	3	4	1	2	4	1	21
All	253	205	80	131	32	49	19	16	15	4	7	1	406
No. of deaths	0		80		64		57		60		37		298
% all deaths	0		27		21		19		20		12		100

*5 died in every case, except one of a family of 10 in which seven people died.

Expected frequencies rounded to nearest whole number, hence totals may not be exact sums of constituent frequencies.

Source: Family reconstitution forms as specified in note 37.

Table 3 shows the results of a set of calculations of this kind, using the appropriate death rate for each family size, taken from Table 2. The columns headed 'Expected' show the numbers of families with 0,1,2... etc. deaths that one would expect given an independent random distribution of burials between families. The columns headed 'Observed' show the numbers of families which recorded 0, 1, 2 ...etc. deaths. The discrepancies between the expected and observed frequencies- are brought out more clearly in Table 4, in which the observed frequencies are expressed as a ratio of the expected frequencies. A ratio of 1.00 means that the same number of burials was observed as would have been expected under independent random conditions. A ratio of 2.00 indicates an observed frequency which is twice the expected frequency, a ratio of 0.50 an observed frequency half the expected frequency, and so on.

Table 4   Ratio of observed to expected frequencies ($\pm$ 0.005)

Size of family	No. dying in family						Chi-square	Degrees of freedom	Probability
	0	1	2	3	4	5 and above			
1	1.00	1.00	—	—	—	—			
2	1.03	0.92	1.56	—	—	—			
3	1.12	0.49	2.01	12.50	—	—			
4	1.40	0.47	0.84	2.55	25.00	—			
5	1.64	0.86	0.20	0.92	7.41	25.00			
6	2.24	0.40	0.23	0.93	7.46	12.50			
7	2.12	0.54	0.49	1.06	2.53	7.69			
8+	4.15	0	0.44	0.70	0.51	4.94			
All	1.23	0.61	0.65	1.21	3.69	6.54	97.68	5	< .001

Source: Table 3, with expected frequencies accurate to 2 decimal places.

A glance at Table 4 shows that the grouping of deaths by family was very different from what one would expect on the basis of an independent random allocation. For every family size the number of families with extreme experiences (no-one dying; everyone or almost everyone dying) was greater than expected, and the number of families with some people dying and others surviving was correspondingly far fewer than expected. There was therefore a marked tendency for deaths to cluster in some families, and for other families to escape the epidemic altogether. Although the numbers of cases are too small for tests of statistical significance to be meaningful for individual family sizes, taken together the patterns are so consistent and strong that it is extremely unlikely that they represent a fluke sample from a population in which burials really were randomly distributed between families.[41]

Thus in Colyton in 1645-6 an individual's chance of dying in the epidemic was not independent of what happened to others in the same family. Furthermore, if the FRFs can be considered to give an approximate, although imperfect, indication of household size, his chance of dying had little, if anything, to do with the size of household in which he lived. If our hypothetical arguments associating different patterns of mortality with different modes of transmission of diseases are correct, then this combination of a strong clustering of deaths with little apparent association between mortality and household size, suggests that the Colyton epidemic is unlikely to have been caused either by an airborne disease or by a contagious disease such as dysentery. It also casts doubt on diseases, such as typhus, which are spread by human parasites. Rather it points to a disease whose distribution is largely determined by ecological factors, and the most promising candidate would seem to be bubonic plague with the rat flea as the significant vector.

Our next concern must therefore be to check our identification of plague by comparing other aspects of the Colyton mortality with what occurred in known outbreaks of bubonic plague. We shall consider three characteristics of plague mortality: the interval between deaths from successive waves of infection, and the distributions of deaths by sex and by age. We shall examine this last point at some length, because the age incidence of epidemic mortality needs calculating with some care.

For bubonic plague spread by the rat flea, Shrewsbury has estimated that the various times required for the transmission of the disease from rat to man for the development of a fatal illness imply an interval between deaths from successive onslaughts of a plague of about fourteen days.[42] When Leslie Bradley tested this estimate against the intervals between burials occurring in the same family in Eyam he found a fair spread of intervals between five and fifteen days, with intervals of between ten and twelve days predominating.[43]

Table 5   Interval in days between deaths in the same family

Interval in days	Frequency	%	Interval in days	Frequency	%	Interval in days	Frequency	%
0	14		10	4		20	3	
1	16		11	9		21	1	
2	7		12	3		22	0	
3	10 ⎯⎯		13	2		23	1	
		39	14	2		24	1	
4	3		15	3		25	1	
5	5		16	2		26	1	
6	5		17	5		27	0	
7	6		18	5 ⎯⎯		28	1	
8	4				51	29	2 ⎯⎯	
9	3		19	0				9

Total under 30 days		119
30 days and above		26

Source: Family reconstitution forms as specified in note 37.

Table 5 shows the distribution of intervals between burials in the same family in Colyton, after excluding intervals of more than thirty days as referring to deaths from unrelated causes. A large proportion of the intervals (almost 40%) were very short, between zero and three days, and these probably relate to deaths occurring with different individual incubation periods after infection from a common source. If we disregard these intervals we find no concentration on or around a particular interval, although intervals of five to seven days, or ten to twelve days as at Eyam, are slightly more frequent than others. The intervals at Colyton therefore seem to be consistent with those observed during a known outbreak of bubonic plague.

When we come to consider the second aspect of plague mortality, its incidence by sex, we are in some difficulty because there does not seem to be any clear-cut pattern reported in the literature. Although Hirst states that 'More cases are reported among males than females', Pollitzer emphasises the variations that occur between epidemics and ascribes them to differences in the exposure of the sexes to infection.[44] Certainly our two seventeenth century English outbreaks differed in this respect: at Eyam both sexes were affected alike, while at St Botolph's far more men than women died.[45] Colyton was more like Eyam: the sex ratio of burials during the epidemic was 93.7 males per 100 females, very close to the sex ratio of 92.9 for the pre-crisis decade from 1633 to 1642.[46]

With the age incidence of plague, however, we have a better chance of a critical test, because a number of medical authorities have written on the subject. For example, Hirst writes that 'The largest number of cases occur in persons between the ages of ten and thirty-five years, the very young and elderley being comparatively little affected.[47] Pollitzer reports that 'in the experience of most observers the incidence of plague was highest in adolescents and in adults up to the age of about forty-five years'.[48] Pollitzer, however, also cites some epidemics in which the distribution of cases by age was rather different and concludes that 'the rule is not invariable', remarking, as with the sex incidence of plague, that differences between epidemics may merely reflect differences by age in exposure to infection.[49] So far as case mortality is concerned, Hirst writes that 'children aged five to ten years showed the lowest mortality and pregnant females, who almost invariable abort, the highest'.[50] Since we have data on the age incidence of deaths in the plague epidemics at Eyam and St Botolph's, our first task must be to discover the age incidence of plague epidemic mortality in seventeenth century English conditions.

There are two methods we can employ to estimate the age-specific incidence of crisis mortality. The most direct, and most satisfactory, way is to calculate properly observed death rates for each age-group during the crisis and compare them with similarly calculated rates obtained for a period of years before the crisis. Unfortunately these calculations are laborious and very prone to error if carried out by hand. The second method is much simpler and quicker: the age incidence of the crisis mortality is estimated by comparing the numbers of burials at different ages both during and before the crisis. Both methods identify 'epidemic mortality' simply as the excess mortality occuring during the crisis over and above the normal level. In this context the term 'epidemic mortality' refers to all the deaths in the crisis period, not just to those caused by the epidemic disease in question. I will discuss the second, simpler, method first, because it raises some fundamental questions about what we mean by the age incidence of an epidemic disease, or the age incidence of epidemic mortality.

First of all, when we compare the numbers of burials at different ages during a crisis with the numbers recorded during a normal period, we must allow for the different lengths of time involved. I have chosen to standardise the numbers of burials recorded in each period by expressing them as an annual frequency. Thus if 223 burials were registered in a period of 10 years before a crisis, and 130 burials in the 13 months the crisis lasted, the equivalent annual frequencies would be 22.3 and 120.0, for the pre-crisis and crisis periods respectively. Secondly, for ease of exposition, I have combined the results for men and women. Very little information is in fact lost by this summary way of proceding, because even at St Botolph's where the overall death rate was higher for men, the age pattern of deaths was much the same for the two sexes.

Table 6   **Excess crisis mortality by age: St Botolph's without Bishopsgate, London 1603**

Age	'Annual' Pre-crisis burials (1600-03)	'Annual' Crisis burials	Recorded excess (2)-(1)	Calculated age-structure	Expected excess burials	Excess ratio (3)÷(5)
	(1)	(2)	(3)	(4)	(5)	(6)
0—4	64	678	614	13	338	1.82
5—14	10	732	722	23	597	1.21
15—44	35	1102	1067	48	1247	0.86
45+	41	236	195	16	416	0.47
All	150	2748	2598	100	2598	1.00

Source: Hollingsworths, *Population Studies,* 1971, Table 2 (burial frequencies), Table 8 (age structure).

If we have a register like St Botolph's, in which ages at burial are recorded for 97% of the entries, the quick and simple method is very quick and simple indeed. Column 1 of Table 6 shows the annual numbers of burials recorded for each age-group in the three years before the epidemic of 1603. I have combined some of the age-groups for which the Hollingsworths originally reported their results in order to make their figures as comparable as possible to Leslie Bradley's figures for Eyam, which I shall discuss below. Column 2 of the Table shows the equivalent annual frequencies of burials recorded during the six months of the plague epidemic. By subtracting the pre-crisis frequencies (column 1) from the crisis frequencies (column 2) we obtain (in column 3) an estimate of the excess numbers of burials due to the epidemic, both generally and for each individual age-group.

Naturally it will only be a rough estimate, because in subtracting the pre-crisis *number* of burials we are assuming that the population remains the same size during the epidemic. This is unlikely to be true, and insofar as the population declines we shall be subtracting too many burials from the observed frequencies and therefore underestimating the 'excess' mortality due to the crisis. It is also quite likely that the age-structure of the population may change during a crisis, because of age-specific differences in migration, or because the epidemic may strike different age-groups with different force, the very question we are trying to investigate. But if this is the case we shall be subtracting too many 'normal' burials from the age-groups most affected by either emigration or mortality, and we shall therefore under-estimate the 'excess' mortality in those age-groups. Conversely we shall subtract too few 'normal' burials from the age-groups relatively lightly affected by emigration or mortality, and we shall overestimate their 'excess' mortality. So this way of proceeding will give con-servative results: we shall both underestimate the general level of excess mortality, and minimize the differences between the excess mortality of the various age groups.

The figures in column 3 of Table 6 show that the crisis mortality during the plague months in St Botolph's was massively greater than normal, and that the greatest number of excess burials accrued to young adults in the age-group 15-44. This is precisely the age-group which the medical authorities single out as having the greatest number of cases of plague. But do the relative *numbers* of cases of plague, or the relative *numbers* of burials, at different ages give any guide at all to the age-specific incidence of plague? Clearly this is not necessarily so, because the numbers of cases of burials recorded for a particular age-group depend not only on the chances of people of that age either contracting the disease or dying from it, but also on how many people there are of that age in the population. Thus the small numbers of plague cases, or burials, recorded for the very young and very old may merely reflect the fact that there are relatively few people of those ages in the population, and tell us nothing about their chances of catching the disease or of dying from it.[51]

Ideally, therefore, we need to know the number of people at risk in each age-group, before we can say anything meaningful either about the incidence of bubonic plague by age, or about the age-specific incidence of epidemic mortality. Unfortunately, in historical epidemics we usually have no way of discovering *how many* people were alive in each age-group, but we can make a rough estimate of the *percentage* of the population in each age-group. We can do this because under theoretically 'stable' conditions the age-structure of a population is determined by the prevailing levels of fertility and mortality, principally the former.[52] In reality both age-specific migration and sudden changes in vital rates may distort the picture, and usually we have no means of assessing how important either of these two disturbing factors may have been. Although we clearly cannot rule them out, we shall proceed here as if they were of no account, because we shall be drawing only very gross conclusions from our theoretical calculations.

If we take levels of fertility and mortality suitable for the seventeenth century, we can obtain from stable population tables the percentages of the population in each age-group given in column 4 of Table 6.[53] We still do not know the actual number of people in each age-group, so we cannot calculate age-specific burial rates. But we can easily test a simple hypothesis such as: 'Epidemic mortality affected each age-group equally', because in this case the distribution of the 'excess' burials in the epidemic would simply reflect the age distri-bution of the population. Fortunately, once again the method is proof against changes in the age-structure of the population occurring during the course of the epidemic. For if some age-groups were more badly affected than others, the true proportion of the population in these age-groups would be less than we have estimated, and we should be expecting too many burials from them. Conversely we should expect too few burials from age-groups which were relatively lightly affected by the epidemic. So when we compare the numbers of burials recorded during the epidemic with the numbers we expect for each age-group, we shall again err on the conservative side of minimising rather than maximising any differences there may be in the age-specific incidence of the epidemic.

In St Botolph's there were 2598 'excess' annual burials during the crisis, and column 5 of Table 6 shows the numbers of burials we would expect to find in each age-group if we were to assume an equal incidence of the epidemic for all ages, and allocate the excess burials simply according to the numbers of people in each age-group. This hypothetical distribution of the 2598 epidemic burials by age is very different from the age distribution actually observed during the crisis and recorded in column 3 of the Table. The deviation of the observed frequencies from those expected on the basis of our 'equal incidence' hypothesis is given in column 6 of the Table. The ratio between the observed and the expected frequencies for the whole population is, naturally, 1.00, for the same 2598 burials are in question. But the ratios for the individual age-groups are very different and they differ systematically with age, being highest for the under-fives and lowest for those aged 45 and above.

Our quick and simple method has enabled us to make two important points about plague mortality at St Botolph's. Firstly that, although the age-group 15-44 has the largest *number* of epidemic burials, it is very far from being the age-group most affected by epidemic mortality. Secondly, it is by no means the case that all age-groups suffered equally in the epidemic: the youngest suffered most and thereafter the impact of epidemic mortality declined with age.

Before we can apply the same method to the burials recorded in the epidemics at Eyam and Colyton we need to deal with the problem of burials of people whose age is unknown. Since neither register records age at burial, the age has to be calculated from a baptism entry linked to the burial record in the course of family reconstitution. If a baptism entry is missing, then the age at burial is unknown. We cannot simply exclude these burials, because in practice they almost all relate to two particular age-groups in the population: children who die before they can be baptised, and adults who move into the parish, usually at, or soon after, marriage.

In his study of Eyam Leslie Bradley avoided the problem of classifying adult burials of unknown age by having a single adult age-group: '20 and above'. He classified the child burials for which no age could be calculated as 'not stated', but I have allocated them to the infant and child age-groups: 0, 1-4, 5-9 and 10-19 in the following manner.[54] Under stable conditions of fertility and mortality the distribution of burials by age also stabilises and can be calculated from the levels of fertility and mortality that obtain. Not knowing the local levels of fertility and mortality at Eyam I took those that had been observed for Colyton in the mid-seventeenth century (expectation of life at birth of 42.5 years and a Gross Reproduction Rate of 2.25) and found the distribution of burials by age in a corresponding model stable population.[55] Despite the apparent arbitrariness of my selection of a model population, the age distribution of burials that it gave was similar to that recorded at Eyam in the pre-crisis period. According to the model population burials under age 20 would be distributed between the age groups 0, 1-4, 5-9, 10-19 in the proportions: .45, .33, .12, and .10.

Table 7   Excess mortality by age; Eyam 1665-6

Age	'Annual' Pre-crisis burials 1651-64 (1) (U)	'Annual' Crisis burials (2) (U)	Recorded excess (2)-(1) (3)	Model age-structure (4)	Expected excess burials (5)	Excess ratio (3)÷(5) (6)
0	6.0 (0.9)	21.1 (8.6)	15.1	3	6.4	2.36
1–4	4.4 (1.1)	25.6 (10.6)	21.2	10	21.4	0.99
5–9	1.6 (0.9)	28.8 (8.6)	27.2	11	23.6	1.15
10–19	1.4 (0.0)	48.8 (0.0)	47.4	20	42.9	1.10
20+	12.2	115.6	103.4	56	120.0	0.86
All	25.6	239.9	214.3	100	214.3	1.00

Note: Figures in columns 1(U) and 2(U) show the allocation of child burials of unknown age.

Source: Bradley, 'Plague at Eyam', above, Table X.

Accordingly I divided the burials of unknown age so that the *total* number of burials in the 'child' age-groups, including the burials of known age, attained these proportions. In the pre-crisis period there were only 2.9 'annual' burials to be allocated and, as column 1(U) of Table 7 shows, they were split fairly evenly between the age-groups 0, 1-4 and 5-9, none needing to be allocated to the age-group 10-19. During the crisis period, however, the normal age pattern of deaths was obviously badly disturbed, so a similar division of the burials of unknown age between these age-groups at first sight seems inappropriate. But whatever method we adopt will influence the results of our comparison between the crisis and the pre-crisis period. In the circumstances it might therefore be best to strengthen the 'equal age-incidence' hypothesis and allocate the crisis burials of unknown age in the same, roughly equal, proportions that obtained in the pre-crisis period. Although this is an arbitrary procedure, it is less likely to exaggerate differences in the epidemic mortality of individual age-groups than if we were simply to allocate all the burials of unknown age to the infant age-group.

The results of applying the same calculations as were made for St Botolph's to the Eyam burials are shown in Table 7. Column 6 of the Table suggests that the age-specific incidence of mortality at Eyam was much the same as at St Botolph's. There is the same fall in the severity of epidemic mortality with age, and of all the age-groups the adults are the least, not the most, likely to die. Although we cannot distinguish between young and old adults, the finer age division of the under-fives shows that, despite our fairly even allocation of the burials of unknown age, the 1-4 year olds escaped relatively lightly, while the infants suffered by far the highest epidemic mortality of all.

In calculating similar figures for the burials recorded during the Colyton epidemic, I have accepted the allocation of child burials of unknown age as recorded on the FRFs. Following the normal rules of family reconstitution a burial entry of a child with no corresponding baptism entry is assumed to refer to a child which died shortly after birth, unless the intervals between the putative date of birth and the date of baptisms of other children in the family are too short, say, less than ten months, or unless the interval between the putative date of birth and the date of baptism of the next oldest child is suspiciously long, suggesting that the burial refers to a rather older child. In allocating the adult burials of an unknown age I have followed the same sort of procedure as I adopted with the child burials of unknown age at Eyam. Using the same model population table I found that deaths over age 20, were divided between the two age-groups, 20-49 and 50+, in the proportions 35:65. Accordingly I again divided the adult burials of unknown age so that the total number of burials in each age group, including the burials of known age, stood in this ratio. For the crisis period I have tried to allow for an element of normal mortality persisting through the epidemic by allocating the same numbers of burials of unknown age to the two adult age-groups as I had allocated in the pre-crisis period. I have also once again tried to strengthen the 'equal age-incidence' hypothesis by allocating the remaining adult burials of unknown age, notionally due to the epidemic, in proportion to the numbers of people alive in each of the two age-groups.

Table 8   Excess mortality by age: Colyton 1645—6

	'Annual' Pre-crisis burials 1633-42 (1)	(U)	'Annual' Crisis burials (2)	(U)	Recorded excess (2)—(1) (3)	Model age-structure (4)	Expected excess burials (5)	Excess ratio (3)÷(5) (6)
0	7.1		26.8		19.7	3	8.8	2.24
1—4	7.6		37.8		30.2	10	29.4	1.03
5—9	2.7		39.7		37.0	11	32.3	1.15
10—19	3.8		68.3		64.5	20	58.7	1.10
20—49	9.7	(5.0)	110.5	(47.4)	100.8	40	117.5	0.86
50+	15.0	(9.4)	56.5	(19.4)	41.5	16	47.0	0.88
(20+)	(24.7)		(167.0)		(142.3)	(56)	(164.5)	0.87
All	45.9		339.6		293.7	100	293.7	1.00

Note: Figures in columns 1(U) and 2(U) show the allocation of adult burials of unknown age.
Source: Family reconstiution forms, all burials.

I have indicated the numbers of burials of unknown age that I have allocated to each of the two adult age-groups both for the crisis and for the pre-crisis period in brackets after the entries for these age-groups in columns 1 and 2 of Table 8. The figures for the pre-crisis period are taken from 1633-42 to avoid the high mortality of 1643-5. But the age pattern of the crisis mortality is so marked that essentially the same picture emerges whatever years are included in the pre-crisis period.

The results of the same set of calculations for the Colyton epidemic are shown in column 6 of Table 8, and they are very close to the Eyam results shown in column 6 of Table 7.[56] Not only is the general pattern of the force of epidemic mortality declining with age the same, but the actual figures for each age-group are almost identical. Also, as is clear from Table 9, when the Colyton figures are adjusted to refer to the age-groups used in the St Botolph's study, the same general pattern emerges, though the mortality levels at Colyton are not so extreme in the case of the very young and the very old.

Table 9 'Excess' crisis in Colyton (1645-6) and St Botolph's without Bishopsgate (1603)

Age group	St Botolph's	Colyton
0–4	1.82	1.31
5–14	1.21	1.12
15–44	0.86	0.92
45+	0.47	0.86
All	1.00	1.00

Source: Tables 6 and 8

Our quick and simple method of measuring the age incidence of epidemic mortality has found a pattern at Colyton remarkably similar to those recorded for two known outbreaks of bubonic plague in seventeenth century England. It has also suggested that the actual age-specific incidence of mortality in a plague epidemic in seventeenth century England was rather different from what might be inferred from hasty reading of medical reports of the age distribution of *numbers* of cases. Specifically it suggests that this epidemic mortality was *less* serious amongst young adults than amongst children, and that infants suffered very much more than other age-groups.

One difficulty with the quick and simple method we have employed is that it makes a number of assumptions which may or may not be true in reality. Our confidence in the validity of our conclusions would therefore be increased if we could show that a direct calculation of age-specific mortality during the epidemic produces essentially the same results.

Age-specific mortality rates are conventionally calculated in two rather different ways. One, known as m_x, relates the number of deaths occurring amongst the members of a particular age-group to the number of years lived in that age-group. This rate is analagous to the more familiar age-specific fertility rate, in which the number of children born to women in a certain age-group is related to the number of years lived in that age-group. In order to be able to calculate an age-specific death rate we need to know the age at burial and so we must confine our attention to those who were baptised in the parish. Since the propensity to migrate varied with age, the death rates we calculate for the very young will be based on the experience of almost every one in the population, while those calculated for the old will be based on a minority of those alive at those ages. Fortunately the information contained on the FRFs allows us to determine exactly how many days each individual lived in each age-group, and whether or not he died. In practice, however, not everyone who appeared on an FRF was in observation all the time, because some left the parish, for example to go out into service. I have tried to minimize the risk of counting individuals as being in observation when they have emigrated by including them in the calculations only if the whole 'family' to which they belong appeared still to be residing in the parish at the beginning of the period being studied.[57] This rule will not be foolproof, especially for those aged between fifteen and twenty-five who may have left the parish to go into service. If they had no burial entry I assumed that they were still resident and alive, and in consequence I may have somewhat underestimated the mortality of the 10-19 age-group. This will be much less true of the 20-49 age group because once individuals were married, generally in their mid-twenties in Colyton at this period, they were usually less mobile and remained in observation on the FRFs.

Table 10   Age-specific mortality (m_x) in Colyton ($\pm$ 0.05)

| Age group | Pre-crisis (1633–42) | | | Crisis (Nov. 1645 – Nov. 1646) | | | 'Excess' Rate |
| | Years lived | Deaths | Rate (2) ÷ (1) x 1000 | Years lived | Deaths | Rate (5) ÷ (4) x 1000 | (6) – (3) |
	(1)	(2)	(3)	(4)	(5)	(6)	(7)
0	739.0	71	96.1	27.1	29	1070.5	974.4
1–4	2608.9	75	28.7	156.6	32	204.3	175.6
5–9	2768.5	26	9.4	190.3	41	215.5	206.1
10–19	4243.9	33	7.8	378.0	62	164.0	156.2
20–49	5325.4	31	5.8	540.8	50	92.5	86.7
50+	1177.1	41	34.8	95.5	24	251.3	216.5

Source: Family reconstitution forms as specified in note 37.

Table 10 gives the age-specific death rates (m_x), expressed as deaths per 1000 years lived, for two periods: the crisis period from November 1645 to November 1646, and a ten year period of more normal mortality running from 1633 to 1642. Once again I have avoided including the years 1643-5 in my 'normal' period, because of their higher than average mortality, and once again the results are strong enough to show up even if these years are taken as the basis for comparison.

By subtracting the normal death rates of the pre-crisis period (column 3) from the crisis period rates (column 6), we obtain an estimate of the age-specific impact of the mortality attributable to the epidemic conditions (column 7).[58] The most striking feature about the figures in this column is how similar the pattern is to the one we obtained by the quick and simple method. Infants are by far the worst affected. Thereafter, apart from the age-group 1-4 years, the epidemic death rates decline with age, until we reach the age-group 50+, when the rate rises substantially higher.than that experienced by the younger adults. This last feature was scarcely evident in the results of the quick and simple method (Table 8), probably because the allocation of burials of unknown age was deliberately biassed against finding an age difference of this kind.

The age-specific death rate recorded for infants during the epidemic is spectacularly and misleadingly high for the purely technical reason that many died very soon after birth, before they could contribute many days to the denominator of the expression used to calculate the death rate. An alternative method of calculating an age-specific death rate, which avoids this difficulty, is to find the proportion of individuals entering an age-group who die before they are old enough to enter the next age-group. Unfortunately almost all of the usual age-groups (0, 1-4, 5-9, 10-14 etc.) are longer than the thirteen months of the Colyton crisis, so I have had to depart from the normal rules for calculating this measure, which is known conventionally as q_x. Also the epidemic occurs at a fixed point in time, so instead of waiting until an individual reaches a certain age before counting him as being 'at risk' in a particular age-group, I have counted him at risk in the appropriate age-group as soon as the epidemic begins, moving him up into another age-group if he crosses the age boundary during the course of the epidemic. Thus the death rates I have calculated for these age-groups during the epidemic give the probability of dying within a thirteen month period, and so are not immediately comparable with conventional q_x rates which give the probability of dying during the full span of the age period.[59] Since the pre-crisis period of ten years is long enough for individuals to live through the full five-year age periods, I have deflated the pre-crisis death rates proportionately so that they are comparable with the thirteen month rates calculated for the crisis period. To emphasise the non-standard nature of my measure I have called it d_x, rather than q_x, and to facilitate comparison with earlier results, I have combined the five-year age-specific rates into the broader categories used in earlier tables.

Table 11   Age-specific mortality (d_x) in Colyton ($\pm$ 0.05)

	Pre-crisis (1633—42)			Crisis (Nov. 1645 — Nov. 1646)			
Age group	At risk	Deaths	Rate* (2) ÷ (1) x 1000	At risk	Deaths	Rate (5) ÷ (4) x 1000	'Excess' Rate (6) — (3)
	(1)	(2)	(3)	(4)	(5)	(6)	(7)
0	860	71	82.6	75	29	386.7	304.1
1—4	928	75	21.8	185	32	173.0	151.2
5—9	848	26	6.6	236	41	173.7	167.1
10—19	1283	33	5.5	457	62	135.7	130.2
20— 49	1633	31	4.1	634	50	78.9	74.8
50+	371	41	23.8	126	24	190.5	166.7

* Rates corrected to refer to a 'crisis length' period as follows.   Source: Family reconstitution forms as specified in note 37.
    1-4: rate x 394/1461
    5-year age groups 5-9 and above: rate x 394/1826.25

Table 11 is laid out in the same format as the previous table giving the results of the m_x rates, and column 7 shows the age-specific death rates (d_x) attributable to the epidemic. As expected the figure for infant mortality is much reduced, but it is still the highest of all and the Table repeats the same pattern of epidemic mortality declining with age, until it rises in the 50+ age-group We have now obtained essentially the same results from two different methods of calculating age-specific mortality, and from a very different quick method of comparing the age-distributions of numbers of burials. We may reasonably conclude that the age pattern of mortality we have observed is a real and marked feature of the Colyton epidemic. The fact that very much the same age pattern appeared in the bubonic plague epidemics at Eyam and St Botolph's strengthens our identification of plague as the disease behind the Colyton epidemic, and suggests that we may have delineated a characteristic age-profile of epidemic plague mortality in seventeenth century England.

Table 12   Infant mortality and parental mortality

Parental mortality	At risk	Infants Dying	Rate ‰
Both die	1	1	1000
Husband survives, Wife dies	9	8	889
Husband dies, Wife survives	13	9	692
Both live	47	11	234
All	70	29	414
Wife dies (rows 1 & 2)	10	9	900
Husband dies (rows 1 & 3)	14	10	714

Source: Family reconstitution forms as specified in text and note 37.

But it by no means follows that this profile represents the age-specific incidence of bubonic plague itself. For deaths in a plague epidemic may be due to a number of causes besides the plague bacillus. Indeed the heavier mortality of the very young suggests that the disruption to normal life that a plague epidemic entailed may have affected those in a dependent situation particularly severely. The information tabulated in Table 12 shows that the death of a parent markedly affected an infant's chance of survival. The table is based on infants whose parents were both alive at the start of the epidemic, and their overall mortality rate was 414 per thousand. But if their father died in the epidemic their mortality rate jumped to almost double this figure at 714 per thousand, while if their mother died, they too were almost certain to die. Yet even when both parents survived the epidemic the infant mortality rate was still more than twice its pre-crisis level. This suggests that something other than the close physical dependency of the infant on its parents affected its chances of surviving the epidemic.

One possibility, which would also help explain the higher mortality of the over 50s, might be that an individual's chance of surviving epidemic conditions of such severity depended partly on physical development and strength. Interestingly enough the higher mortality of the over-50s observed at Colyton was conspicuously absent at St Botolph's, where this age-group was the least likely to die. Since St Botolph's, as a London parish, will have experienced endemic plague over many years, we may here be observing a special case in which the regular fall in epidemic mortality with age partly reflects a progressively greater immunity to plague amongst the higher age-groups. In Colyton, where endemic plague is unlikely to have occurred, the disease will have fallen on an epidemiologically virgin population. In these circumstances the relative physical strengths of different age groups may have influenced their chances of surviving not only the plague, if plague it was, but also the rigours and hardships connected with the upheaval in normal life brought about by an epidemic of this magnitude.

In the thirteen months between November 1645 and November 1646, when the burial register could finally record 'here the siknes ended', about a fifth of the inhabitants of Colyton had died. There can be no certain identification of the 'siknes', but the overwhelming balance of the evidence is in favour of a verdict of bubonic plague. Although the late November start and the persistently high, though not excessive, mortality of the winter months are unusual features of a plague epidemic, they are not incompatible with the disease, and the massive summer peak of burials, dying away in the autumn of 1646, follows the classic seasonal pattern of plague. Furthermore, the extreme localisation of the epidemic in Colyton, the marked clustering of deaths in certain households, and the apparent lack of connection between the level of mortality and household size, all point to a disease spread by an animal-borne vector such as the rat flea, rather than an airborne or contagious disease, or one spread by human parasites. Finally the age distribution of the epidemic mortality in Colyton is remarkably similar to that found in two known seventeenth century outbreaks of bubonic plague.

Although we can never hope to describe the full impact of an epidemic of this severity on the lives of the inhabitants of Colyton, we have been able to discover at least some of the dimensions of its incidence. We have observed how some age-groups suffered very much more than others, and how these age-groups were not those singled out in the medical literature as experiencing the highest 'incidence' of plague. We have also seen that deaths clustered in families, so that, despite the high mortality, no less than 62% of the families escaped death entirely.[60] Unfortunately the uninformative character of the Colyton register at this point prevents us from discovering whether the mortality was concentrated amongst families of a specific social status, or confined to particular localities. But the complete absence of any sign of an epidemic in the surrounding parishes argues for some geographical concentration, probably in the larger settlements of Colyford and Colyton town.

If we consider the set of social rules and attitudes that affected the life chances of the inhabitants of a seventeenth century community, we might deduce that the force of the impact of an epidemic on the social fabric will have depended considerably on the age and marital status of those who died. In a world in which the young and unmarried occupied a dependent status, the more the epidemic fell upon the 'full' members of the community, breaking up married couples or eliminating them altogether, the greater the social and economic dislocation will have been. Indeed for the young who needed access to a landholding or craft workshop in order to gain their economic independence and so marry, epidemic mortality may have opened up economic and domestic opportunites which otherwise might have taken years to materialise.

In order to gauge the impact of the epidemic mortality on the social and economic fabric of Colyton, we need to restrict our attention to those families in which both spouses were still alive at the start of the epidemic. Table 13 shows for the 324 couples in observation the number of cases in which both partners died, both survived, or either the husband or the wife alone survived.

Table 13   Mortality of married couples

	Number	%
Both survive	236	73
Husband survives, Wife dies	31	10
Husband dies, Wife survives	38	12
Both die	19	6
Total couples	324	100

Source: Family reconstitution forms as specified in text and note 37.

In the overwhelming majority of cases (73%), the family as a social and economic unit comprising two adults survived intact, and in only 6% was it eliminated altogether in the epidemic. Thus there were only 19 openings for newly married couples. In a further 69 cases the family was functionally impaired by the death of either the husband or the wife. Although in principle these circumstances provided an opportunity for bachelors or spinsters, it is remarkable how seldom in practice the surviving spouse remarried. Of the 31 widowers only 9 (29%), and of the 38 widows only 3 (8%) remarried. But since only a further 15 of the widowers and 9 of the widows are known from a later burial entry to have remained unmarried in the parish after the epidemic, it is possible that the other 7 widowers and 26 widows may have left the parish, thereby freeing 33 further holdings for others to occupy. However this may have been, there was no sudden surge of marriages either during or immediately after the epidemic. Indeed very few marriages were registered until 1650, after which the numbers of marriages were markedly lower than those recorded in the years before the epidemic, and the pre-crisis level was only regained at the very end of the eighteenth century. Baptisms, but not burials, also plunged to a much lower level after the crisis, and here the pre-crisis level had not been regained by 1830. Tony Wrigley's reconstitution of the register has shown that these aggregative movements reflected decisive changes in the underlying patterns of nuptiality, fertility and mortality.[61] After the plague, women, but not men, married much later, and marital fertility was deliberately reduced, while the general background level of mortality remained high for all ages. But not all these changes can be ascribed to the epidemic. The change in background mortality was part of a more long-term shift towards higher levels in the seventeenth century, which is discernible in other places besides Colyton.[62] And it is possible that fertility had already begun to decline, though without any evidence of conscious control, before the epidemic began.[63] Finally, how far either the rise in the age at marriage of women, or the appearance of family limitation, can be linked to the experience of the epidemic must remain a matter of conjecture.[64] But the severity of that experience and the magnitude of the demographic changes that followed are beyond all doubt.

APPENDIX

Characteristics of Common Diseases

Disease	Age group affected	Season	Case fatality rate	Length of epidemic	How transmitted
Diphtheria	mostly 2-5	mostly winter	usually < 10%, can reach 40%	variable	airborne
Dysentery	sometimes very young only	summer/ autumn	2% - 40%	variable	food etc. contaminated by contagion, flies
Influenza	normally severest on old	winter and early spring	normally < 1%, 1918: 6-13%	2-3 months	airborne, with 8% - 50% infected
Measles	mainly children	cooler months	< 1%, up 10% die of pneumonia	variable	airborne
Plague (bubonic)	all	spring— November	60% - 80%	variable	rat flea, less frequently human flea
Plague (pneumonic)	all	winter	c. 100%	usually <3 months	airborne
Scarlet fever	mainly 1-9	summer/ autumn	usually < 4%	variable	airborne
Smallpox	mainly children	any, usually winter	c. 30%	variable	airborne, occasionally contaminated food
Typhoid (enteric fever)	all	autumn	15% - 20%, increasing with age	variable	polluted water and food
Typhus	all	winter/ spring	10% - 20%, can reach 50%	variable	lice, rarely airborne
Whooping cough	80% < 5, 11 girls per 9 boys	winter/ spring	variable, infants 20%	2-3 months	airborne

This appendix summarises a number of characteristics of some common diseases which caused epidemic mortality in pre-industrial England. In practice epidemic outbreaks show great variation, and the highly simplified and grossly generalised information tabulated here should be used with caution. It is based on a similar table published by Dr C.D. Rogers in *The Lancashire population crisis, 1623,* Manchester University Extra Mural Department, 1975, and I am very grateful to Dr Rogers for allowing me to make use of his work, which was based on W. Ostler and T. McCrae, *The principles and practice of medicine.* The table presented in this appendix is a revision of Dr Rogers' table in the light of additional information from the *British encyclopaedia of medical practice,* 2nd edition.

Acknowledgements

Many people have helped me write this chapter. Les Pepper prepared most of the tables from Tony Wrigley's Family Reconstitution Forms and typed the manuscript. Oly Anderson edited and ran my computer programs. Roger Sellman provided me with information about the burial frequencies recorded in the registers of a large number of Devon parishes, and Paul Slack gave me information about mortality in the wider region of the south-west. Paul Slack, Derek Turner, Christopher Charlton and Leslie Bradley made valuable comments on earlier drafts and saved me from several errors of fact and judgement. Finally Tony Wrigley has helped and advised me at every stage of my research.

Notes

1. E. A. Wrigley, 'Family limitation in pre-industrial England', *Economic History Review,* 2nd ser., XIX, no. 1, 1966; 'Mortality in pre-industrial England: the example of Colyton, Devon, over three centuries', *Daedalus,* Spring 1968, reprinted in D. V. Glass and R. Revelle, eds., *Population and social change,* 1972; *Population and history,* 1969.
2. See, for example, T. H. Hollingsworth, *Historical demography,* 1969, pp. 185-95; J.D. Chambers, 'Some aspects of E.A. Wrigley's "Population and History", *Local Population Studies,* no. 3, Autumn 1969.
3. Wrigley, *Econ. Hist. Rev.,* 1966, p.85.
4. Mary Hollingsworth and T. H. Hollingsworth, 'Plague mortality rates by age and sex in the parish of St Botolph's without Bishopsgate, London, 1603', *Population Studies,* 25, no. 1, March 1971, pp.131-46. Leslie Bradley, 'The most famous of all English plagues', earlier in this volume.
5. The Colyton register is still in the parish church. The SSRC Cambridge Group for the History of Population and Social Structure holds a xerox copy of the register from its inception until 1837.
6. David Levine, 'De-industrialisation and changing marital habits in Colyton', *Local Population Studies,* no. 13, Autumn 1974, p.52.
7. Paul Slack, 'Some aspects of epidemics in England, 1485-1640', D.Phil. thesis, Oxford, 1972, ch. 2.
8. John Rushworth, *Historical collections,* VI, 1701, p.94.
9. Joshua Sprigge, *Anglia rediviva,* 1647, pp.145-6. Page references are to the 1854 edition. An unnumbered.front page states that Sprigge was chaplain to General Fairfax. C. Walker in his *Compleat history of Independency,* 1660-1, p.53, claims that *Anglia rediviva* was really written by Colonel Fiennes of the New Model Army.
10. Sprigge, *Anglia rediviva,* p.146. There is a convenient table of the army's movements on p.335.

11. *ibid.*, p.167.
12. *ibid.*, p.122-3.
13. Creighton noticed the different fortunes of the two armies at Tiverton in 1644 and 1645. C. Creighton, *A history of epidemics in Britain*, 1891, reprinted 1965, I, pp. 552-5.
14   Sprigge, *Anglia rediviva*, p.167.
15. Devon County Record Office, Devon Quarter Sessions Order Book, 1640-51, entries under the months stated in the text. Information and reference supplied by Paul Slack.
16. Devon: Branscombe, Chardstock, *Clyst, *Culmstock, *Feniton & Harpford, Hemyock, Ottery St Mary, *Sidmouth, Topsham, *Uffculme, *Yarcombe. Somerset:Crewkerne , Pitminster. Figures for asterisked parishes supplied by Paul ·Slack, others from aggregative analyses with the Cambridge Group.
17. The registers of Axmouth, Dalwood, Farway, Musbury, Offwell, Seaton and Beer, and Widworthy were kindly analysed for me by Dr. Roger Sellman, The registers of Northleigh, Southleigh and Shute are missing for this period.
18. The Exeter wheat price series is often reproduced. See, for example, B. R. Mitchell and P. Deane, *Abstract of British historical statistics*, Cambridge, 1971, pp.484-7.
19. T. Short, *A comparative history of the increase and decrease of mankind*, 1767, reprinted 1973, p.84.
20. Short describes a large number of ailments as common in these years, *ibid.*, p.91.
     1728:   'Fevers, Quotidians, Tertians, Quartans, Remittents, putrid, spotted.'
     1729:   'Chincough, Rheumatisms, Inflammations and a general scabbiness. All low grounds sore afflicted with obstinate Quartans and Tertians. At Plymouth Rheumatisms, Arthritis, suffocating coughs, fatal to the Asthmatic and Consumptive. In May inflammatory Fevers and Chicken-Pox; in June Erysipelas and Small-Pox; in July a putrid Fever, Itch and Scabbiness, in November a universal catarrh.'
     Short himself was a practising doctor at the time. Although he lived in south Yorkshire he was in correspondence with colleagues elsewhere, probably including Dr John Huxham of Plymouth, whose Diary is discussed in *Local Population Studies*, no. 12. Spring 1974, pp.34-5.
21. Based on parish register analyses supplied by Dr Roger Sellman. All but one of the city parishes experiencing epidemic mortality did so in 1729, one parish in 1728 and 1729, and one in 1730 only. Epidemics in the rural parishes were more evenly spread over the years 1727-1732, with 10 of the 16 parishes which experienced epidemics doing so in 1729.
22. Materials available at the SSRC Cambridge Group for the History of Population and Social Structure.
23. The parishes are Grantham, Lincs; Melton Mowbray, Leics; Mancetter, Warwicks; Wymondham, Norfolk; Hadleigh and Woodbridge, Suffolk; Gravesend and Milton-next-Gravesend Kent; Colyton, Devon. The years involved are 1563, 1604(2), 1631, 1637 (2), 1646, 1666 (2). With the exception of 1646 (Colyton), these are all known plague years; in every case the mortality peaks in the summer, and in some cases there are explicit references to plague in the registers.
24. Unless the population is confined to a small space, as in a siege, infection rates of more than 50% of the population are rarely reported in medical literature. See, for example, *British encyclopaedia of medical practice*, 2nd ed., 1952, under the name of any communicable disease.
25. *Encyclopaedia Britannica* (1970), under 'Influenza', Of several thousand cases treated at a military hospital in England during the same pandemic, between 6% and 8% died. *The Lancet*, 1919, 1, p.1.

26. Hollingsworths, *Population Studies*, 1971, Table 2, p.135.

27. Bradley 'Plague at Eyam', above, Table X.

28. The identification, which appears to be correct, is that of G. E. Evans, a late nineteenth century local historian. Curiously, Evans misdates the annotations to 28 November 1645 and 22 December 1646. G. E. Evans, *Colytonia: a chapter in the history of Devon*, 1898, pp.4,7.

29. See Appendix 1.

30. See Appendix 1; Biraben, 'Current medical and epidemiological views on plague' and Bradley, 'Some medical aspects of plague', above .

31. The distribution of intervals between burials in the same family is discussed below.

32. For the influence of climate on the activity and longevity of fleas, see Biraben, 'Current views', above.

33. I owe the information about London to Roger Finlay. See, for example, the plague of 1624-5 in A.W.C. Hallen, *The registers of Botolph's without Bishopsgate, 1558-1753*, 1886-95. For Sweden see O.T. Hult, *Pesten i Sverige, 1710*, Stockholm, 1916, especially pp. 50-1, 69, 100-3. For a remarkable contemporary doctor's description of the spread of plague through the winter in the small town of Norrköping, illustrated by detailed case notes, see Magnus Gabriel Block, *Atskillige anmärkningar öfwer närwarande Pestilentias Beskaffenhet*, Linköping, 1711.

34. M. Baltazard, 'Epidemiology of plague', *World Health Organisation Chronicle*, 14, no.11 Nov. 1960, pp.419-26. I owe this reference to Andrew Appleby.
    In Stockholm and other Swedish localities in the autumn of 1710 it was observed that deaths from plague increased when the sky was overcast and a southerly wind was blowing, and decreased when the wind came from the north and the skies were clear. Hult, *Pesten i Sverige*, p.101.

35. See any elementary statistics textbook; for example M. J. Moroney, *Facts from figures*, (Pelican) 1953, pp. 88-95.

36. P. Laslett, 'Mean household size in England since the sixteenth century', in P. Laslett and R. Wall, eds., *Household and family in past time*, Cambridge, 1972.

37. A family was in observation if it was formed (date of marriage or date of baptism of first child) before the beginning of the epidemic and if at least one parent was still alive at the beginning of the epidemic. A stricter rule was also tried which required both parents to be alive at the start of the epidemic. This made no difference to the results, so the original slacker rule was followed in order to increase the number of FRFs studied. The few families which were formed during the epidemic were also included.

38. But if children were born during the epidemic they were counted in determining family size.

39. Of the 403 burials registered during the crisis period (Table 1), 35 appear to refer to migrants or temporary residents and so were not included on the FRFs. Of the remaining 368 burials, 70 were excluded through the observation rules specified in note 37, leaving the 298 burials recorded in Table 2.

40. For an elementary discussion of random variation and the precision of sample estimates see R. Schofield, 'Sampling in historical research', in E. A. Wrigley, ed., *Nineteenth century society*, 1972.

41. The most convenient measure of statistical significance, chi-square, requires a minimum expected frequency of five in any one cell. The numbers of FRFs for most family sizes are so small that to achieve this we would have to amalgamate adjacent cells where the observed frequencies were much more, and much less, than expected, and in so doing we would obliterate the clustering pattern. The overall chi-square statistic has

been calculated by summing the observed and expected frequencies for each column over all rows (family sizes). These totals are somewhat hybrid figures, again amalgamating cells with frequencies above and below expectation. But the final chi-square statistic, for all its imperfections, represents a probability of less than one in a thousand that the observed frequencies reflect an independent random allocation of burials to families.

42. J. F. D. Shrewsbury, *A history of bubonic plague in the British Isles,* 1970, p.3.

43. Bradley, 'Plague at Eyam', above, Table IX, column B.

44. L. F. Hirst, 'Plague', in *British encyclopaedia of medical practice,* 2nd ed., 9, 1952, p.61; R. Pollitzer, *Plague,* 1954, pp.503-4.

45. Bradley, 'Plague at Eyam', above, Table X; Hollingsworths, *Population Studies,* 1971, pp. 144-5.

46. Pre-crisis period: 221 male and 238 female burials. Crisis period: 178 male and 190 female burials.

47. Hirst, 'Plague', p.61.

48. Pollitzer, *Plague,* p.504.

49. *Ibid.*

50. Hirst, 'Plague', p.73.

51. Note that this question of the age-structure of the population is logically distinct from Pollitzer's point about age or sex differences in the degree of exposure to infection.

52. For a succinct introduction to stable population theory, see Hollingsworth, *Historical demography,* Appendix 1.

53. In fact these percentages were calculated by the Hollingsworths correcting stable population theory with estimates of migration. Hollingsworths, *Population Studies,* 1971, p. 138-44. They are very close to the percentages used later for Eyam and Colyton, which are taken from a stable population with a 'North' pattern of female mortality, an expectation of life at birth of 42.5 years, and a gross reproduction rate of 2.25, tabulated in A. J. Coale and R. Demeny, *Regional model life tables and stable populations,* 1966. The levels of fertility and mortality are from Tony Wrigley's family reconstitution of Colyton, see the references in note 1. For an alternative approach which uses stable population theory to recover the same levels of fertility and mortality for Colyton from aggregative frequencies, see R. Lee, 'Estimating series of vital rates and age structures from baptisms and burials: a new technique, with applications to pre-industrial England', *Population Studies,* 38, no. 1, 1974.

54. In a personal communication Leslie Bradley told me that his impression is that these burials relate to young children.

55. Coale and Demeny, *Model life tables,* as specified in note 53.

56. If the pre-crisis period is taken to run from Jan. 1643 to Oct. 1645, the figures in column 6 of Table 8 read: 2.17, 1.14, 1.22, 1.21, 0.76, 0.90, (0.80).

57. See note 37.

58. If the pre-crisis period is taken to run from Jan. 1643 to Oct. 1645, the figures in column 7 of Table 10 read: 875.7, 166.8, 198.6, 152.8, 72.0, 175.7.

59. Those who cross an age boundary during the epidemic will spend less than thirteen months in each age-group, but, hopefully, the gains and losses will even out between the age-groups.

60. That is 253 out of 406 families; see Table 3.

61. Corroborated by R. Lee's article cited in note 53.

62. The Cambridge Group has family reconstitution studies of nine other parishes of widely differing social and economic characteristics, scattered over the whole country, which all show this pattern.

63. The cohort married 1630-46 has rather lower age-specific marital fertility rates than the previous cohort, but without the 'concave' pattern exhibited by the rates of the subsequent cohort. Wrigley, 'Family limitation' (as in note 1), Table 4, p.89.
64. David Chambers explores this argument in the article cited in note 2.

The Geographical Spread of Plague

Leslie Bradley

The growing interest in the historical plague epidemics in this country has, up to the present, largely centred on the degree of plague mortality and the consequent economic and social effects, and comparatively little work has been done on questions relating to the transmission of the disease between communities. The first step in the discussion of transmission must be the plotting of geographical locations and the apparent dates of the arrival of plague in the various communities over a suitable region. The London plague of 1603, for example, appears to have originated in Stepney. When and in what order did it reach the surrounding parishes and how did it spread northward from the urban parishes? Creighton, of course, recorded the locations and, though sometimes imprecisely, the dates of many local outbreaks. It is perhaps surprising that, though the recent edition of his book[1] has made his work so much more accessible and familiar, and though in the last few years parish registers and other local records have been so extensively used for demographic purposes, there have been so few attempts at epidemic plotting. Here is a very useful field to be explored by local historians. It has its difficulties, especially when one tries to pass from purely factual plotting to an attempt to describe the mechanism of plague transmission. It is the purpose of this chapter to discuss these difficulties.

The London plague of 1603 will be used as an illustration. No complete survey has been made, but the data used here were collected in a limited investigation of the incidence of the disease along the road northward from London to Ware and Hertford.[2] The Table shows the monthly incidence of burials in the London parishes in which the epidemic is reputed to have started and in a number of parishes on or near the road to Ware. In four of these parishes the date of the first plague burial is known from the parish register, in one other the month but not the day of the first plague burial is given, whilst in the others the month of the start of the epidemic (assuming the ascription to plague to be correct) has had to be inferred, as explained below, from an increase in the number of burials. The Figure plots these dates roughly in accordance with the geographical locations of the parishes.

TABLE
Monthly burial totals 1603

	Jan	Feb	Mar	Apl	May	Jun	July	Aug	Sept	Oct	Nov	Dec	Total	
Stepney all burials	24	15	37	49	44	71	318	597	673	289	93	51	2261	
plague burials				8	3	29	266	572	630	269	84	31		
St. Botolph's without Aldgate	20	20	24	37	62	118	433	667	349	120	36	20	1906	Plague not mentioned
St. Botolph's without Bishopsgate	18	13	17	11	21	95	465	559	233	59	20	27	1538	Plague not mentioned
Whitechapel	13	19	22	17	35	146	465	650	384	114	46	24	1935	Register says plague began May
Clerkenwell	9	9	6	13	12	8	88	339	251	43	13	10	801	Plague not mentioned
Islington	1	5	8	3	7	6	25	70	101	73	28	4	331	Plague not mentioned
Bow all burials	1	2	5	0	3	1	2	12	30	32	18	10	116	
plague burials							1	10	24	15	16	6		
Hackney	5	6	5	6	7	6	36	89	95	42	12	13	322	First plague entry July 8th
Stoke Newington	0	0	2	0	2	0	9	4	16	10	5	3	51	Plague not mentioned
Tottenham	2	0	0	3	1	3	5	4	14	15	15	6	68	
Edmonton all burials	12	5	9	3	5	2	4	6	28	38	20	13	145	First plague entry Aug. 23rd
plague burials								3	22	24	17	9		
Enfield	7	9	4	7	5	0	9	38	56	46	48	25	254	First plague entry July 7th
Waltham Holy Cross	5	2	12	3	4	1	3	3	9	18	15	12	87	Plague not mentioned
Cheshunt	3	4	10	6	9	9	12	41	30	15	15	6	160	First plague entry June 19th
Ware	1	4	6	14	5	8	8	23	25	18	16	13	141	Plague not mentioned
Hertford	6	2	2	2	2	3	2	1	8	9	17	18	72	Plague not mentioned

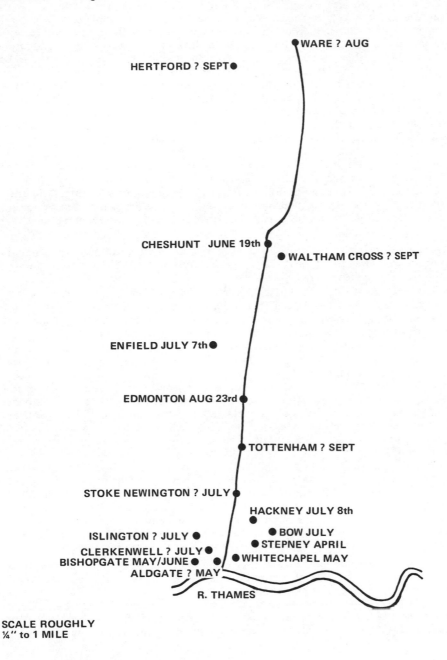

Occurance of Plague north of London May to September 1603.

WARE ? AUG

HERTFORD ? SEPT●

CHESHUNT JUNE 19th ●

● WALTHAM CROSS ? SEPT

ENFIELD JULY 7th●

EDMONTON AUG 23rd ●

● TOTTENHAM ? SEPT

STOKE NEWINGTON ? JULY ●

HACKNEY JULY 8th
●

ISLINGTON ? JULY ●   ● BOW JULY

CLERKENWELL ? JULY●   ● STEPNEY APRIL

BISHOPGATE MAY/JUNE ●   ● WHITECHAPEL MAY

ALDGATE ? MAY

R. THAMES

SCALE ROUGHLY
¼" to 1 MILE

129

The epidemic appears first in Stepney in April and the records show it a month later in Whitechapel and in the two City parishes of St. Botolph's without Aldgate and St. Botolph's without Bishopsgate. The next surge of burials occurs in June, one month later, at Cheshunt, some thirteen miles up the road to Ware. In July the epidemic appears to have spread both south from Cheshunt to the parish of Enfield and north from the City to the neighbouring parishes of Clerkenwell, Islington, Hackney and Bow. In August the records show it to be in Edmonton, the parish immediately to the south of Enfield, and in September the gap between this northern group of parishes and the group immediately surrounding the City is closed when the epidemic appears in Tottenham. In August the epidemic is revealed in Ware and in September it has tracked west to Hertford. The plague of 1603 thus appears to have radiated out from London, and quite early seems to have reached Cheshunt which became a secondary source of infection. But is this a valid interpretation of the data?

Tracing the detailed route of an epidemic involves placing in a time-sequence the dates at which the *causative agent* arrived at each of the affected communities. Is this possible for an English plague epidemic? It is one thing to plot the geographical location of surges of burials and quite another thing to make statements about the transmission of the causative agent. The available records are bills of mortality, parish registers and contemporary diaries or similar documents.

1. Bills of mortality, which exist only for a relatively small number of parishes, mainly in the larger towns, give the date of burial and the cause of death. The date of the first plague *burial* in an epidemic can be established.

2. Parish registers give the date of burial. In a few of them plague deaths are specifically designated, so that again the date of the first plague burial can be established. In the majority, however, the cause of death is not stated and this raises two problems, that of recognising a plague epidemic and that of dating the first plague burial.

   a. Unusually high monthly burial totals indicate an epidemic - but of what? Plague? Smallpox? Influenza? Typhus? Shrewsbury[3] suggests that when a parish register shows an excessive number of burials in a year and a monthly analysis reveals that ✓more than fifty percent of them is contributed by any three successive months of the plague period, June to October inclusive, the record is suggestive of an outbreak of plague in the parish; if this contribution rises to sixty-six percent he regards the ascription as almost certain. This, the only rule which, so far as I know, has been suggested, still leaves some identifications in doubt (for example Waltham Holy Cross and Hertford).

   b. In the absence of stated cause of death we would normally identify as the first plague month that in which the number of burials first rises significantly above the average for that month of the year, but we still do not know whether the *first* plague burial occurred early or later in the month or, indeed, whether it could not have occurred in the previous month (as, for example, in Bow and Edmonton). It seems therefore that although in some parishes the first plague burial can be dated, in the majority of cases there is an uncertainty which may be as much as three or four weeks.

3. Diaries and other contemporary records may, if reliable, give the date of the first plague burial or, even better, the date of the onset of illness in the first victim, but such information is available for very few parishes indeed.

The position, then, is that in a minority of parishes the date of the first plague burial, or in exceptional cases of the first onset of illness, can be determined but that in the majority of cases there is considerable uncertainty. And to this we must add an uncertain period between the arrival of the causative agent and the first burial, for

1. even if the first victim is immediately infected, as he may be if the vector is a human flea, there is an incubation period which may vary from one to six days[4] and a period of illness which may last for only two or three days but may extend considerably longer[5].
2. if the human infection is consequent on a rat epizootic we may have to add several more days.[6]

It is evident then that the uncertainty in dating the arrival of the causative agent in the affected community is such as to make the establishment of a reliable time-sequence difficult or impossible (except, as suggested below, in large towns) and without this it is impossible to trace the detailed sequence of the spread of the plague epidemic.

The position may be different in the populous parishes of a large town. Even if there are no bills of mortality, the large number of cases and the frequency of intercourse between parishes statistically lessen the uncertainty in timing so that it is often possible to trace the progress of the epidemic from its original focus as, for example, in the case of the London parishes from the focus in Stepney.

The argument so far has been based on the difficulty of timing the arrival of the causative agent, but even if this could be done with reasonable accuracy there is a further problem. The tendency is to take as a model the spread of a highly contagious disease and to expect a fairly simple outward progress from the original focus. This cannot be expected for plague if the spread was due to the transport of fleas or rats either on the person or in merchandise.[7] If a traveller leaving an infected town carried infective fleas (and it must be remembered that only a minority of *infected* fleas are *infective*[8]) he could travel up to some twenty-five miles in the course of a day. At which stop in the course of the day, or even of two or three days, he shed a flea is a matter of chance. Even if every flea carried from the town started an outbreak of plague (and this would most certainly not be so) chance would play a large part in determining the geographical distance at which successive outbreaks were caused, and the time-space distribution of the outbreaks would not usually be a simple outward progression. The same is true if the infection was carried by rats or fleas harbouring in merchandise. Finally if, in England, infection was carried by field rodents rather than by commensal rats or by fleas we have to reckon with 'the capricious nature of these epizootic trails'.[9]

What of an exodus from an infected town? According to Creighton, by the end of May 1603 there was a royal proclamation commanding gentlemen to depart the court and city on account of the plague[10] and he also asserts that the Hertfordshire villages were favourite resorts of Londoners in times of plague.[11] Those in a position to flee the city would be likely to have contacts already established at varying distances over a considerable area, so that their movement would be rather random in pattern. Thus only in the case of a mass panic exodus would the refugees engulf first the nearest and then progressively the more distant villages. Once again, the exception will be for the spread of infection between the parishes of a large town, though even here the infection could 'jump' - the second parish to be infected after the Stepney focus need not be one of those immediately adjacent to Stepney.

Conclusion

It is, of course, possible to make certain very general statements such as that plague tends to travel along lines of communication and that, over considerable distances, plague tends to arrive later at places more distant from the original focus, though even here it has to be remembered that there may be more than one focus and that a rat epizootic dormant during the winter may revive an epidemic without a fresh infection. Apart from such general statements, detailed discussion of the way in which plague spread in the historical epidemics is difficult. A reliable time-sequence can only be established for a minority of affected parishes and even then it does not necessarily establish a causative sequence. Much more work is needed in this field and it is to be hoped that local historians will start the process by undertaking the necessary preliminary regional plotting.

Notes

1. Charles Creighton - *A History of Epidemics in Britain*. 1894. Second edition, Frank Cass 1965.
2. By Mr. Tom Lewis, to whom I am indebted for the parish register aggregates.
3. J.F.D. Shrewsbury - *A History of Bubonic Plague in the British Isles*, Cambridge.1970, p. 175.
4. Medical Aspects of Plague, p. 16
5. Ibid. p. 13 and p. 16
6. Ibid. p.16
7. Ibid. p.15
8. Ibid. p.14
9. Ibid. p.16
10. Op.Cit. p. 481
11. Op.cit. p. 493

Plague and the General Reader

A Review of non-specialist writing on the Plague

Derek Turner

Whilst historical demography may seem to be a narrowly specialist subject to the general reader - and to some professional historians who should know better - most people have heard of and think they know something about the plague, in particular the Black Death. It is a subject considered to be of sufficient general interest for the mass media to have broadcast not only a play but a documentary about the notorious plague visitation of Eyam in 1666 (more accurately described elsewhere in this volume). Alert viewers of the programme, if such there be, may have registered surprise at the date. Most likely they were taught that the 'Great Plague' came in 1665 and the 'Great Fire of London' in 1666 put an end to it. Their teachers, in the unlikely event of being challenged as to their omniscience by a pupil from Eyam or one of the many other English settlements plague-ridden in 1666, could have quoted in their defence no less an authority than Trevelyan in *England under the Stuarts* to the effect that 'after 1665 England knew it (the Plague) no more'[1], and Maurice Ashley who in the Pelican history of England also implies that the Plague ended in 1665 and that the Great Fire had something to do with its disappearance [2]

That the Plague ended in 1665 is a simple error of fact, that the Great Fire was a cause of its disappearance is a historical judgement which few present-day specialist historians believe to be the whole truth. There are mistakes in Trevelyan and Ashley because they wrote some years ago, yet their books are readily available in bookshops and libraries and are likely to be consulted by the educated reader or viewer stimulated by television or a chance entry in his local parish register into wishing to know more about the Plague. What chance has he of being provided by writers of general histories with reliable and up-to-date information and judgements about the history and epidemiology of the Plague? Do recent general works incorporate the findings of modern historical and medical scholarship, or is today's general reader fed with the stale myths and half-baked theories that have characterised most writing about the Plague for the last six hundred years or more?

To answer these questions with reference to all the relevant general works of history and textbooks over the whole plague era would be a massively tedious operation. The scope and limitations of this survey can be described as follows. I have chosen to look only at those books or part of them which deal with the 1348-9 and 1665-6 plagues but I have taken note of any references to the other fourteenth or sixteenth/seventeenth century plagues. I have been guided in my selection of works not by their scholarly rating but by the likelihood of their being consulted by the general reader searching the shelves and catalogues of his local town or county library. I have therefore selected standard works and the most recently published general histories. I have also included some reference to recent school textbooks on the supposition that just as modern parents struggle to understand the 'New Maths' from their children's textbooks, so they may turn hopefully to a secondary school history book for enlightenment about the Plague.

Overall, the results of my survey have been disheartening. I have learnt a great deal more about how textbooks are written - or should I say patched together - than about the Plague. Notwithstanding the enormous advances in the study of social and economic history in recent decades, general histories are all too often still stuck in well defined political ruts and give scant attention to the hard facts of social history or to consideration of their importance. There are however some hopeful signs amongst the more recently published textbooks or general histories that there is growing a new awareness of social history and demography.

In assessing the books I have tried as far as possible to withhold my own judgement as to the correctness of the views expressed on matters which are still the subject of controversy amongst specialists, such as the extent of the plague mortality of 1348-9, but I have noted carefully whether the writer admits the existence of doubt and controversy and whether he gives references; for nothing is more frustrating to the newly keen amateur historian, hot on the trail, than to be met by a wall of silence as to how the information so smoothly presented was obtained.

The palm for the most misleading description of the Black Death and the Great Plague must go to Trevelyan, though he has two points in his favour. He does refer to Creighton, at the time he was writing the most eminent authority on plague epidemics. Also, he refers to the Great Plague as 'the last but *perhaps not the worst* (my italics) of a series of outbreaks covering three centuries.' It is perhaps for this latter reason that his description is praised by Ian Sutherland as 'an excellent summary' in his own recent work, 'When was the Great Plague?' (in *Population and Social Change*, edited by D.V. Glass and Roger Revelle, London 1972). Yet this 'excellent summary' includes the claim that 'it is not improbable that half the subjects of Edward III perished within three years' and that 'the obscurest hamlet had little chance of escape.' 'Until 1665', he continues, 'the Black Death remained in the soil of England.' It is not clear whether the reader is to take this literally or metaphorically. In the forty years between the publication of *England under the Stuarts* and *English Social History* [1] little has changed. The relevant passages are virtually identical though a footnote now adds that in 1665 plague was 'not quite confined to London.' Despite Sutherland's recommendation, Trevelyan in any form is, in the phraseology of the consumer magazines, a 'bad read'.

The heavy weight and sombre hard covers of the volumes of the Oxford History of England exude a ponderous air of authority. In May McKisack's *Fourteenth Century* [3] the reader is given his money's worth. Five pages (out of 532) contain quite a detailed account of the spread of the Black Death across England, distinguish between the bubonic and pneumonic forms of plague and consider its immediate and wide ranging impact in some detail. McKisack alleges that the Black Death claimed the older and more prominent people. She quotes Russell's mortality figures of twenty percent for 1348-9 and fifty percent by the end of the century [35] She reviews the evidence of mortality from the episcopal registers, claiming dubiously that 'about half the clergy fell victim to the plague' and refers to Hamilton Thompson, Coulton and Renouard. [28,23,33] She also quotes several local examples of high mortality from Boucher, Fisher, Robo and Levett [22,26,34,29] but rightly stresses that mortality levels were uneven. She admits that few 'lost' villages can be directly linked with the Black Death but claims, without revealing her authority, that Tilgarsley (Oxon.), Middle Carlton and Ambion (Leics.) were such villages. She emphasises that the Plague caused no general panic and only a temporary disruption in the wool-trade. Nevertheless she lists as results of the plague: falling prices, labour shortage, increased leasing of demesne, while admitting that on the whole landlords found no great difficulty in finding tenants for vacant holdings. She believes that shortage of labour and rising wages coupled with a serious cattle disease led to social disturbances in the generation following the Black Death. The main trend of her argument is that the more significant effects were gradual and delayed rather than immediate and cataclysmic. 'A generation or so later (than 1348-9) the effects, other than the immediate effects of this disaster, were *beginning to be perceptible*' (my italics). 'Black Death' but not 'Plague' appears in the index.

The working methods of one brand of textbook writer is nowhere better illustrated than in a comparison between McKisack's work, first published in 1959, and a recent school textbook of medieval history from a reputable publisher which appeared in 1973. Denis Richards and Arnold E. Ellis devote two pages to plague out of 283 in a book which covers Britain 400 -1485. [4] The whole section is taken almost word for word from McKisack but the detailed examples which add colour to her account are omitted. The later plagues are mentioned as less virulent. In a gratuitous excursion beyond the confines of their chosen period the authors continue, 'Thereafter plague was a recurrent visitor, casting a deep shadow over late Tudor times, and ending only with the epidemic known as the Great Plague.' It looks very much as though the inspiration for this passage came from Trevelyan. Once again, through the uncritical acceptance of glib generalisations, the sufferings of Eyam are as though they had never been. One cannot ask of writers of school textbooks that they be widely read on all aspects of a thousand years of British history yet one might reasonably expect them not to lean so heavily upon a single twenty-year-old standard work. Historical accuracy apart, it is doubtful whether watered-down Oxford history is an ideal way to present the Plague - or any other history for that matter - to schoolchildren.

Fortunately it is clear that some modern textbook writers do at least take the trouble to write in their own words. From the same publisher comes another book. *The Middle Ages* by R.J. Cootes [5], even more ambitious in the ground it attempts to cover but nevertheless devoting two pages out of 198 to the Black Death. The epidemiology of plague, its spread across Europe and Britain and its demographic effects are all briefly but fairly accurately described. In a laudable attempt to bring the subject alive for children, historical imagination sometimes threatens accuracy. 'No part of England escaped entirely; dead bodies littered roads and fields all over the countryside.' In the interests of brevity or simplicity dubious assertions are made about the cause and effect. 'In time people must have developed some resistence to it (the Plague) because later outbreaks were mild compared with 1348.' The chapter-heading 'Black Death and Peasants Revolt' will encourage children to link the two in simple cause and effect. Despite these blemishes, the almost unavoidable result of the compression needed in a text book of this type, this book provides a lively and reasonably accurate account of the Black Death.

The best example of what a good recent textbook can offer is given by M.H. Keen in *The Later Middle Ages*.[6] Writing for sixth-formers and covering a briefer time-span, he can of course spread himself more. Maurice Keen is a scholar of some distinction and although no expert on this particular aspect of the later middle ages, he has used his scholarly training to good effect. He gives the usual description of the 1348-9 and later fourteenth century epidemics. About the level of mortality he is duly cautious. The 1348-9 plague 'may have killed a third of the population.' He stresses the uneven incidence of mortality, referring to the work of Page, Beresford and Levett.[31,21,29] He also emphasises the difficulty of interpreting the evidence of the episcopal registers, quoting with approval Bean and Ziegler[19,17] and referring to Hamilton-Thompson and Shrewsbury.[28,37] He considers the rival population estimates of Postan and Russell[35,32] and includes a long footnote on the controversy over the size of medieval population, concluding, 'the central incontrovertible fact remains however that there was a dramatic contraction of the population as a result of the plagues of the middle of the fourteenth century.' On the mortality of the Black Death in particular he examines the claim by Shrewsbury that the aetiology of the Plague excludes the possibility of a mortality as high as the lowest figure suggested by historians, and, referring to Bean and Wu Lien-Teh[19,30] suggests that Shrewsbury has ignored the possibility of the emergence of a pneumonic form of plague which would both explain its survival through the winter and make possible a far higher overall mortality than Shrewsbury's five percent. However, he in turn ignores Shrewsbury's suggestion that the big winter mortality was caused by typhus fever. Whilst he admits that other factors were involved, he states, 'the reduction of population consequent upon the plague affected all aspects of economic life, trade, distribution of urban prosperity, the social and economic structure of the rural world.' All in all this is as good a general account as one could expect to find in a modern textbook, clearly hostile to Shrewsbury's interpretation but fair in referring to sources from both sides in the controversy.

The same cannot unfortunately be said of the latest work by a scholar of much greater public reputation. Professor Postan's *Medieval Economy and Society*[7] makes no attempt at a balanced judgement. This is not a true textbook for its coverage is deliberately patchy and its tone argumentative. The didactic, declamatory approach is nowhere more evident than in Postan's treatment of the Black Death - 'a disaster so unprecedented and so great that it has engraved itself upon the collective memory of Englishmen for many generations to come.' 'The extent of the ravages, though defying all exact measurement, must have been enormous' he writes with scant regard for logic. His supposedly despicable opponents remain unidentified. 'Recent attempts to play down mortality... need not be taken seriously... are based on arguments of no great cogency... Contemporaries would not have regarded an increase of ten or fifteen percent mortality as unusual or catastrophic.' The low figures he believes are at variance with the historical evidence. 'Most of the villages and all of the towns for which we have evidence suffered grievously' he writes but omits any discussion of whether the sample is likely to be representative of the country as a whole. 'Amongst the better historians' (!) he continues, 'some would put mortality at twenty percent, others would put it near forty percent but fifty percent would also not be wholly improbable.' He regards the later outbreaks of the 1360s and 1370s as sufficiently serious to 'have earned for themselves the ill repute and name of Black Death but for memories of 1348.' Unsurprisingly he ignores Shrewsbury's suggestion that the later epidemics were not plague at all. Overall, Postan weakens what could be a strong case by his undisguised prejudice and cavalier handling of the evidence. Unfortunately, librarians, aware of Postan's reputation and of the lack of general books on medieval social and economic history, will be pleased to add this book to their collection.

Postan refers openly only to Saltmarsh, Bean and Titow.[36,19,8] The last of these is another specialist in the field who has - ostensibly - written a book for the general reader. *English Rural Society*[8] is an invitingly slim volume. The blurb states that it is 'aimed primarily... at the newcomer to the subject.' Titow limits his discussion of the Black Death to its immediate demographic effects, a justified curtailment in that his book is concerned with the period 1200-1350. He writes of two very serious outbreaks: '1349-50' (sic) and '1361-2'. He attacks the traditional mortality figure for 1348-9 of one third as too low and Russell's aggregate figure for fourteenth century mortality of forty percent as far too low. Even Postan's fifty percent is 'on the low side.' Similarly a forty percent figure for clerical mortality in 1348 is 'probably much too low'. In support of his own high estimates he quotes a figure of forty-three percent for parts of Essex, fifty-six for the Crowland Abbey estates. No mention is made of the fact that these figures are both derived from East Anglia, where Shrewsbury suggests mortality was much higher than the national average due to the higher density of population. Titow indulges in a lengthy refutation of Russell's evidence and uses his own unpublished figures for the estates of the bishop of Winchester and Glastonbury Abbey, concluding that the most reliable evidence points to a mortality above fifty percent for the rural population. Notwithstanding the blurb's claims, this book can only be handled by specialists and would bemuse and mislead the general reader unfamiliar with other works and views on the Black Death. In this case it is hard to know whether it is the publisher who is at fault, seeking to increase sales by a misleading blurb, or the author who has failed to write the book the publisher or general editor of the series asked for.

If for the fourteenth century the general reader has to contend with prejudice and partiality, for the seventeenth he is likely to be frustrated by silence and apathy. For the typical general historian, demography assumes a momentary importance in the second half of the fourteenth century and again becomes a significant factor in the later eighteenth century. Between these two dates, population history has for him little importance. The mounting population of the sixteenth century is briefly mentioned in connection with the Tudor inflation or the sturdy beggar. The many and varied epidemics of the Tudor and early Stuart period are largely ignored. The Great Plague of 1665 makes a brief appearance traditionally linked with the Great Fire and its only significance seems to be as a contribution to English naval failures against the Dutch! Trevelyan's shortcomings on this topic have been emphasised enough already. Sir George Clark's Oxford history[9], written in an age before more than a handful of historians took social history seriously, writes briefly but well, referring to Creighton and Bell [24,20] but errs in supposing that the Great Plague was the worst epidemic since 1348. He points out that the panic and misery left its mark on literature and touches on the futility of superstitious 'cures' and counter measures that made things worse. It is a human and sympathetic account but lacks any hard demographic information.

The only worthwhile account among general works is to be found in David Ogg's comprehensive *England in the Reign of Charles* II[10]. Ogg gives a detailed account of the plague in London, noting the previously sultry weather, the growing numbers dying, the spread of the plague to the provinces, and names the main cities affected. He identifies plague as a disease of the poor, describes scenes of heroism by the clergy, doctors and magistrates together with remedies suggested by the College of Physicians and the theories and practice of Nathaniel Hodges. He comments on the isolation of healthy people in infected houses and the general lack of government involvement until May 1666. He refers to Defoe's *Chronicle*[25] which 'compensates for historical inaccuracy by imaginative truth'. He also discusses Graunt's use of the Bills of Mortality[27] and concludes that plague caused increased interest in the science of public health and the inauguration of the science of medical statistics. In general there is little to cavil at in this treatment of the Great Plague. The wider issues are ignored as are the reasons for the Plague's disappearance from Britain, an omission understandable in view of the reluctance of even the specialists to deal with these questions.

Sixth-form textbook writers, if Lockyer's well thought of *Tudor and Stuart Britain*[11] is typical, devote little attention to plague. In Tudor times according to Lockyer, 'growing immunity to plague had halted the decline in the population', a generalisation that begs a lot of questions. His description of the Great Plague in London is a precis of Ogg. The reader is given no indication that the Plague occurred in London before 1665 or existed outside the capital. It becomes increasingly clear why school textbook writers still rely on Ogg's forty year old work when one turns to the general histories of the seventeenth century written by modern scholars. This century has become a battleground in which religious, social and economic historians of Marxist and other persuasions have raised clouds of dust that have obscured much uncontroversial historical development. The student of the period, dazed by his mentors' obsession with the rise of the gentry, may be excused for failing to notice the undoubted rise of the population of London from around one hundred thousand to something approaching five hundred thousand between the middle of the sixteenth and the middle of the seventeenth century, despite the recurrent and often serious plague epidemics. One turns in vain to the general histories of the seventeenth century for even the most basic information about the Plague. For Maurice Ashley[2] it is a mere hiatus in the Anglo-Dutch wars. In Christopher Hill's much Praised *Century of Revolution*[12], there is no mention of plague in the index and but two scant references in the text. The first merely refers to the Great Plague's occurrence in 1665. The second reads, 'The disbandment of 500,000 soldiers, the Plague, the Fire of London, the Dutch Fleet in the Medway, all these shook the economy'. If one hopes for more from this author in his social and economic history,[13] this hope soon fades. One learns only that plague was frequent in the seventeenth century with severe outbreaks in 1625 and 1665, that it was extinct by the end of the century and 'did not recur, even in the famine years 1693-99', a statement which, by implicitly making a causal link between famine and the spread of plague, reveals little understanding of the way by which plague was passed on. On the general effects of the Plague, Hill writes, 'Victory over the plague gave stimulus to and confidence in further medical science and created the possibility of a *stable* (Hill's italics) industrial society in urban conglomerations'! This prize piece of historical generalisation involves so many unproved assumptions that the historical demographer's mind boggles, but it is alas all too typical of the casual way in which social and economic historians of the seventeenth century treat demographic topics.

Ironically, while academics have been busy chasing Marxist moonbeams, the Great Plague (and Fire) have been quite well served by the authors of school textbooks, for they are subjects which fulfill the criterion of a 'good story' and conform to the current fashion for social history backed with suitable documents. Thanks therefore to Pepys, Bills of Mortality etc., publishers offer quite a selection of works on the Plague. The best of these are more detailed and more reliable than anything written for adults or sixth-formers, though London remains the sole focus of attention and the Great Plague is for ever linked with the Great Fire. Cowie's *Plague and Fire*[14] is typical of the best of these books. Fifty-eight out of 118 pages are devoted to the 1665 plague. The existence of plague in London before 1665 is briefly referred to but no details are given. A wide range of sources are quoted or referred to: Graunt[27], Evelyn, Pepys, Richard Baxter, Clarendon and Defoe[25]. Bell's *The Plague in London*[26] is used as the basis of the narrative account. Many contemporary or near contemporary illustrations are used. Different chapters describe London in the seventeenth century, the onset, spread and decline of the plague, government countermeasures and the efforts of private individuals.There is little to cavil at in the detail but it is a pity that no real attempt is made to set the London plague in a wider geographical and chronological context. Only a few lines are devoted to the years before and after 1665 and the plague outside London. Cowie's treatment is workmanlike and thorough but - one must add - lacks historical imagination.

Plague and Fire also figure as No.2 in the large and commercially successful 'Jackdaw' series, the first of the now common document packs to be marketed[15]. It consists of five broadsheets covering very much the same ground as Cowie's book but in less detail, and a small number of documents, facsimiles or transcriptions, including a bill of mortality. All these and more are included in Cowie's book though there is some educational advantage in having separate sheets and larger scale reproductions. The text of the broadsheets is sound and some effort is made to put the 1665 plague in its chronological context. For instance the severe London plagues of 1563 and 1625 are referred to. Opinions differ on the educational value of the 'jackdaw' format but this one at least, given its limitations, does no injustice to history.

The same cannot unfortunately be said of Roger Hart's *English Life in the Seventeenth Century*[16], which can be taken as typical of the less good middle school history book. Such a book these days usually has excellent illustrations to accompany a mediocre text. Hart gives rather a haphazard description of the Plague in London before 1665 and includes the quite erroneous statement that the last serious plague before 1665 was in 1630. The description of the plague, countermeasures etc. is quite lively but prone to over-simplification. The belief of Dr. Gumble, who 'saw all the official reports', that 100,000 people died of the plague outside London is reported without comment and with implied approval. It is only from Cowie that one learns that Gumble was physician to the Duke of Albemarle, who was Governor of the City and that the 'official reports' were those sent to Albemarle. With this extra information a student can make some judgement of his own upon the reliability of the figures. Without it he will naturally assume that 'official reports' expressed the truth. Hart, whose book covers Stuart life in general, cannot of course afford to give as many words to the plague as Cowie, and the deficiencies of his treatment are not so much a criticism of his writing as an indication of the short-comings of the history textbook approach. A particular danger here for teachers lies in the fact that Hart's book, well produced, lavishly illustrated and quite expensive, will not be recognised for what it is: an old fashioned textbook in modern dress. Publishers do harm by dressing up their mutton as lamb. Perhaps they themselves, seeing only the glossy paper and the high class illustrations, are the victims of self delusion.

In summary, the general reader would do well to eschew all standard works bar Keen, Ogg and possibly McKisack. On the whole, the medieval historians have made a better attempt than their seventeenth century counterparts to come to grips with specialist works and to recognise the importance of demographic and epidemic history. Moreover, for the seeker after enlightenment about the Black Death, there is a tremendous bonus in the shape of Philip Ziegler's *Black Death*[17], a book written by a layman for laymen but with scholarly attention to sources and evidence. Sadly, it was published just before Shrewsbury's book appeared and was accordingly unable to take into account the latter's important though controversial contribution. Nevertheless Ziegler's book still remains the best answer for students of the Black Death. In addition to a readable and detailed account of all aspects of the Black Death, there is one chapter which gives a fictional but entirely plausible account of the plague striking a village, an account which I know from experience teaches schoolchildren more about the Plague in half an hour than any number of textbooks. No comparable book exists for the Tudor and Stuart plagues, though *Man, Environment and Disease* by G. Melvin Howe[18] gives a sound and up-to-date, if very compressed, account of plague among other diseases over a broad time-span. Those who want more than a brief introduction, whether adult or child, will gain most from the secondary school topic books, which make up in liveliness and use of contemporary sources for what they lack in academic analysis.

One can only conclude that the general reader's book, and indeed the general historian's book on the plague has yet to be published. Until one such appears, the enthusiastic novice who wants something more than a short and often inaccurate answer will have to hack his way through the jungle of specialist works. If nothing else, this survey may serve to warn him against promising looking but unprofitable or misleading lines of exploration and direct him towards those works which, if his enthusiasm persists, will ultimately teach him most of what current scholarship has to say about the history of the Plague in Britain.

Notes

Books and articles mentioned in the text are listed in two sections. The first comprises general historical works, school textbooks and works on plague designed for the general reader. The second section lists those specialist works referred to in the general histories.

1.   G.M. Trevelyan, *England under the Stuarts*, 1904.
                English Social History, 1944.
2.   Maurice Ashley, *England in the Seventeenth Century*, 1952.
3.   May McKisack, *The Fourteenth Century*, 1959.
4.   Denis Richards and Arnold D. Ellis, *Medieval Britain*, 1973.
5.   R.J. Cootes, *The Middle Ages*, 1972.
6.   M.H. Keen, *England in the Later Middle Ages*, 1973.
7.   M.M. Postan, *The Medieval Economy and Society*, 1972.
8.   J.Z. Titow, *English Rural Society 1200-1350*, 1969.
9.   G.N. Clark, *The Later Stuarts*, 1934.
10.   D. Ogg, *England in the Reign of Charles II*, 1934.

11. Roger Lockyer, *Tudor and Stuart Britain,* 1964.
12. Christopher Hill, *The Century of Revolution,* 1961.
13. Christopher Hill, *Reformation to Industrial Revolution,* 1969.
14. L.W. Cowie, *Plague and Fire,* 1970.
15. *Plague and Fire,* Jackdaw No. 2.
16. Roger Hart, *English Life in the seventeenth Century,* 1970.
17. P. Ziegler, *The Black Death,* 1969.
18. G. Melvin Howe, *Man Environment and Disease in Britain,* 1972.
19. J.M.W. Bean, 'Plague, Population and Economic Decline in England in the Later Middle Ages', *Econ. Hist. Rev.* 2nd ser. XV, 1962-3.
20. W.J. Bell, *The Great Plague in London in 1665,* 1924.
21. M. Beresford, *The Lost Villages of England,* 1954.
22. C.E. Boucher, 'The Black Death in Bristol', *Transactions of the Bristol and Glos. Arch. Soc.* LX. 1938.
23. G.G. Coulton, *Medieval Panorama,* 1938.
24. C. Creighton, *A History of Epidemics in Britain,* 1894.
25. D. Defoe, *A Journal of the Plague Year,* 1722.
26. J.L. Fisher. 'The Black Death in Essex', *Essex Review,* LIII, 1943.
27. J. Graunt, *Natural and Political Observations on the Bills of Mortality,* 1665.
28. A. Hamilton Thompson, 'The Pestilences of the Fourteenth Century in the Diocese of York', *Archaeological Journal,* LXXI, 1914.
29. A.E. Levett, 'Studies in the Manorial Organisation of St. Albans Abbey', *Studies in Manorial History,* 1938.
30. Wu Lien-Teh, *A Treatise on Pneumonic Plague,* 1926.
31. F.M. Page, *The Estates of Crowland Abbey,* 1934.
32. M.M. Postan, 'Some Evidence of Declining Population in the Later Middle Ages', *Econ. Hist. Rev.* 2nd ser. II, 1950, and *Cambridge Economic History of Europe;* vol. 1, 2nd ed., 1966, pp. 560-70.
33. Y. Renouard, 'Conséquences et intérêt démographique de la peste noire de 1348', *Population. III.* 1948.
34. E. Robo. 'The Black Death in the Hundred of Farnham', *Eng. Hist, Rev.* XLV, 1929.
35. J.C. Russell, *British Medieval Population,* 1948.
36. J. Saltmarsh, 'Plague and Economic Decline in England in the Later Middle Ages', *Cambridge Historical Journal,* VII, 1941.
37. J.F.D. Shrewsbury, *A History of the Bubonic Plague in the British Isles,* 1970.

Index